A Note From Rick Renner

I am on a personal quest to see a "revival of the Bible" so people can establish their lives on a firm foundation that will stand strong and endure the test as end-time storm winds begin to intensify.

In order to experience a revival of the Bible in your personal life, it is important to take time each day to read, receive, and apply its truths to your life. James tells us that if we will continue in the perfect law of liberty — refusing to be forgetful hearers, but determined to be doers — we will be blessed in our ways. As you watch or listen to the programs in this series and work through this corresponding study guide, I trust you will search the Scriptures and allow the Holy Spirit to help you hear something new from God's Word that applies specifically to your life. I encourage you to be a doer of the Word He reveals to you. Whatever the cost, I assure you — it will be worth it.

> Thy words were found, and I did eat them;
> and thy word was unto me the joy and rejoicing of mine heart:
> for I am called by thy name, O Lord God of hosts.
> — Jeremiah 15:16

Your brother and friend in Jesus Christ,

Rick Renner

Unless otherwise indicated, all scripture quotations are taken from the *King James Version* of the Bible.

Scripture quotations marked (*AMPC*) are taken from the *Amplified® Bible.* Copyright © 1954, 1958, 1962, 1964, 1965, 1987 by The Lockman Foundation. Used by permission. **www.Lockman.org**.

All Scripture marked with the designation (*GW*) is taken from GOD'S WORD®. © 1995, 2003, 2013, 2014, 2019, 2020 by God's Word to the Nations Mission Society. Used by permission.

Scripture quotations marked (*NIV*) are taken from *Holy Bible, New International Version®, NIV®* Copyright ©1973, 1978, 1984, 2011 by Biblica, Inc.® Used by permission. All rights reserved worldwide.

Scripture quotations marked (*NKJV*) are taken from the *New King James Version®*. Copyright © 1982 by Thomas Nelson. Used by permission. All rights reserved.

Scripture quotations marked (*NLT*) are taken from the Holy Bible, *New Living Translation*, copyright © 1996, 2004, 2015 by Tyndale House Foundation. Used by permission of Tyndale House Publishers, Inc., Carol Stream, Illinois 60188. All rights reserved.

Scripture quotations marked (*TLB*) are taken from *The Living Bible* copyright © 1971. Used by permission of Tyndale House Publishers, Inc., Carol Stream, Illinois 60188. All rights reserved.

Scripture quotations marked (*TPT*) are from *The Passion Translation®*. Copyright © 2017, 2018 by Passion & Fire Ministries, Inc. Used by permission. All rights reserved. ThePassionTranslation.com.

Psalm 23: The Lord Is My Shepherd

Copyright © 2021 by Rick Renner
8316 E. 73rd St.
Tulsa, Oklahoma 74133

Published by Rick Renner Ministries
www.renner.org

ISBN 13: 978-1-68031-893-7

eBook ISBN 13: 978-1-68031-894-4

All rights reserved. No portion of this book may be reproduced or transmitted in any form or by any means — electronic, mechanical, photocopy, recording, scanning, or other — except for brief quotations in critical reviews or articles, without the prior written permission of the Publisher.

How To Use This Study Guide

This ten-lesson study guide corresponds to *"Psalm 23: The Lord Is My Shepherd" With Rick Renner* (**Renner TV**). Each lesson in this study guide covers a topic that is addressed during the program series, with questions and references supplied to draw you deeper into your own private study of the Scriptures on this subject.

To derive the most benefit from this study guide, consider the following:

First, watch or listen to the program prior to working through the corresponding lesson in this guide. (Programs can also be viewed at **renner.org** by clicking on the Media/Archives links.)

Second, take the time to look up the scriptures included in each lesson. Prayerfully consider their application to your own life.

Third, use a journal or notebook to make note of your answers to each lesson's Study Questions and Practical Application challenges.

Fourth, invest specific time in prayer and in the Word of God to consult with the Holy Spirit. Write down the scriptures or insights He reveals to you.

Finally, take action! Whatever the Lord tells you to do according to His Word, do it.

For added insights on this subject, it is recommended that you obtain Tony Cooke's book *Because the Lord Is My Shepherd: The Blessings of an Empowered Life* and Rick Renner's autobiography *Unlikely: Our Faith-filled Journey to the Ends of the Earth*. You may also select from Rick's other available resources by placing your order at **renner.org** or by calling 1-800-742-5593.

LESSON 1

TOPIC
God's Supernatural Provision

SCRIPTURES

1. **Psalm 23:1-6** — The Lord is my shepherd; I shall not want. He maketh me to lie down in green pastures: he leadeth me beside the still waters. He restoreth my soul: he leadeth me in the paths of righteousness for his name's sake. Yea, though I walk through the valley of the shadow of death, I will fear no evil: for thou art with me; thy rod and thy staff they comfort me. Thou preparest a table before me in the presence of mine enemies: thou anointest my head with oil; my cup runneth over. Surely goodness and mercy shall follow me all the days of my life: and I will dwell in the house of the Lord for ever.
2. **Isaiah 53:6** — All we like sheep have gone astray; we have turned everyone to his own way....
3. **Luke 15:4** — What man of you, having an hundred sheep, if he lose one of them, doth not leave the ninety and nine in the wilderness, and go after that which is lost, until he find it?
4. **Matthew 6:25-33** — Therefore I say unto you, Take no thought for your life, what ye shall eat, or what ye shall drink; nor yet for your body, what ye shall put on. Is not the life more than meat, and the body than raiment? Behold the fowls of the air: for they sow not, neither do they reap, nor gather into barns; yet your heavenly Father feedeth them. Are ye not much better than they? Which of you by taking thought can add one cubit unto his stature? And why take ye thought for raiment? Consider the lilies of the field, how they grow; they toil not, neither do they spin: And yet I say unto you, That even Solomon in all his glory was not arrayed like one of these. Wherefore, if God so clothe the grass of the field, which to day is, and to morrow is cast into the oven, shall he not much more clothe you, O ye of little faith? Therefore take no thought, saying, What shall we eat? or, What shall we drink? or, Wherewithal shall we be clothed? (For after all these things do the Gentiles seek:) for your heavenly Father knoweth that ye have need of all these things. But seek ye first the kingdom of God, and his righteousness; and all these things shall be added unto you.

5. **Psalm 37:25** — I have been young, and now am old; yet I have not seen the righteous forsaken, nor his seed begging bread.
6. **Deuteronomy 2:7** (*NLT*) — For the Lord your God has blessed you in everything you have done. He has watched your every step through this great wilderness. During these forty years, the Lord your God has been with you, and you have lacked nothing.
7. **Psalm 84:11** (*NKJV*) — For the Lord God is a sun and shield; the Lord will give grace and glory; No good thing will He withhold from those who walk uprightly.
8. **Psalm 103:2-5** — Bless the Lord, O my soul, and forget not all his benefits: Who forgiveth all thine iniquities; who healeth all thy diseases; Who redeemeth thy life from destruction; Who crowneth thee with lovingkindness and tender mercies; Who satisfieth thy mouth with good things....
9. **Philippians 4:19** — But my God shall supply all your need according to His riches in glory by Christ Jesus.

GREEK WORDS

There are no Greek words in this lesson.

SYNOPSIS

The ten lessons in this study on ***Psalm 23: The Lord Is My Shepherd*** will focus on the following topics:

- God's Supernatural Provision
- God's Supernatural Protection
- God's Supernatural Peace
- God's Supernatural Restoration
- God's Supernatural Guidance
- God's Supernatural Confidence
- God's Supernatural Protection and Correction
- God's Supernatural Prosperity
- God's Supernatural Anointing
- God's Supernatural Promise

The emphasis of this lesson:

Just as a shepherd provides for all the needs of the sheep in his flock, Jesus — our Good Shepherd — faithfully provides us with everything we need to live our lives and bring Him glory.

Of all the passages in the Bible, one of the most widely known and loved sections of believers throughout all generations is Psalm 23. Under the unction of the Holy Spirit, David penned these six verses while serving as a shepherd of his father's sheep. He wrote:

> The Lord is my shepherd; I shall not want. He maketh me to lie down in green pastures: he leadeth me beside the still waters. He restoreth my soul: he leadeth me in the paths of righteousness for his name's sake. Yea, though I walk through the valley of the shadow of death, I will fear no evil: for thou art with me; thy rod and thy staff they comfort me. Thou preparest a table before me in the presence of mine enemies: thou anointest my head with oil; my cup runneth over. Surely goodness and mercy shall follow me all the days of my life: and I will dwell in the house of the Lord for ever.
> — Psalm 23:1-6

In this cherished passage, we are provided with ten powerful promises. These include:

1. God's supernatural provision (Psalm 23:1)
2. God's supernatural protection (Psalm 23:2)
3. God's supernatural peace (Psalm 23:2)
4. God's supernatural restoration (Psalm 23:3)
5. God's supernatural guidance (Psalm 23:3)
6. God's supernatural confidence (Psalm 23:4)
7. God's supernatural correction (Psalm 23:4)
8. God's supernatural prosperity (Psalm 23:5)
9. God's supernatural anointing/blessing (Psalm 23:5)
10. God's supernatural promise (Psalm 23:6)

In the coming lessons, we will explore all ten of these promises. In this lesson, we will take a close look at the meaning of David's words in verse 1:

'The Lord is my shepherd; I shall not want.'

It's no surprise that David refers to the Lord as a *shepherd*. His choice of this metaphor was birthed from his personal experience serving as a shepherd and spending a great deal of time caring for sheep as a young man. In other places in Scripture, the Lord is referred to as King, Judge, and Deliverer. But here, in the first verse of the Twenty-Third Psalm, He is referred to as a shepherd.

What Does a Shepherd Do?

A shepherd is a leader and caretaker of the sheep. As he tends the sheep, he feeds them and ensures their basic needs are met. The shepherd also protects the flock from wolves, leading and guiding the sheep where he wants them to go. A shepherd has deep concern and care not only for all his sheep collectively, but also for each one individually.

David declared that this is how the Lord cares for us — He is our *Good Shepherd*. The Bible says He knows each of our comings and goings (*see* Psalm 139:1-6), and He even has a count of every hair on our heads (*see* Luke 12:7). He knows when one of us strays away and gets lost and is mindful of everything that is going on in our lives. And since the Lord is our Shepherd, that makes us His sheep.

What Do We Know About Sheep?

There are eleven specific characteristics that apply to all sheep everywhere.

1. **Sheep can be slow to learn.** Any shepherd can tell you countless stories about how sheep can easily get themselves into a very painful situation and yet fail to learn their lesson from it. For instance, a sheep may get caught in barbed wire trying to break through a fence or fall into a ditch and get stuck. After the shepherd painstakingly rescues the sheep, it is not uncommon for that same sheep to go out the very next day and try the exact same thing again. Sheep are slow learners.
2. **Sheep can be stinky and unattractive.** The typical illustrations of fluffy, white lambs are not as accurate as you might think. Although some shepherds may tell you otherwise, to most outside observers, sheep are dirty, smelly, and ugly.
3. **Sheep are demanding.** Have you ever watched a lamb suckle its mother? Almost as soon as it's born, it begins to violently suck its

mother's udders, and that insatiable demand to be fed never leaves them. As they grow, they demand grass, grass, and more grass — day after day and night after night. When snow is on the ground, they aggressively demand food from the shepherd. If their feeding trough is empty even for a short time, they begin to bleat incessantly. They will even stampede their shepherd when he appears, demanding that he feed them.

4. **Sheep are stubborn.** Have you ever tried to move a sheep? It's like trying to move an elephant. Likewise, if you've ever tried to lead a sheep, you know they can be quite stubborn.

5. **Sheep are strong.** Don't let their skinny "arms" and "legs" fool you. Although you may think sheep will be easy to handle, they can knock you flat! Shepherds have been flattened by running sheep, knocked on their backs and left face down in the dirt. A sheep's head butting is both a natural and learned behavior. The fact is, sheep can be extremely aggressive and have been known to cause serious injuries, even death, to people.

6. **Sheep tend to go astray and get lost.** Jesus Himself alluded to this wandering tendency in sheep. He said, "What man of you, having an hundred sheep, if he lose one of them, doth not leave the ninety and nine in the wilderness, and go after that which is lost, until he find it?" (Luke 15:4). And we are just like sheep. The Bible says, "All we like sheep have gone astray; we have turned every one to his own way…" (Isaiah 53:6).

7. **Sheep are unpredictable.** The moment you think you know the direction sheep are heading, they surprise you and go the opposite way. It's hard to predict what sheep will do!

8. **Sheep tend to follow the crowd.** One observer has said, "When one sheep decides to start running, they will all decide to start running." If you were able to ask one of the sheep, "Why did you start running?" It would say, "Well, because he started running." And every other sheep in the pack would echo the same reason, one after the other. When you got to the last sheep he would just say, "I don't know. I saw all the other sheep running and decided to do the same thing."

Indeed, when one sheep moves, the rest will follow — even if it doesn't seem to be a good idea. The flocking and following instinct of sheep is so strong that it once caused the death of 400 sheep in Turkey. Because one sheep got the bright idea to try and cross a hundred-foot-deep ravine, the 399 sheep accompanying him instinctively chose to follow, and all of them plunged to their death one after the other.

9. **Sheep are restless.** In fact, they are so restless they will continue to roam about into the wee hours of the night searching for food. Similarly, God's people are restless like sheep. It's hard to get them to be still and rest.

10. **Sheep are dependent on a shepherd.** Although many animals can cope and thrive in the wild without any close supervision, sheep cannot. They are totally dependent on their shepherd and cannot live without him. In the same way, as believers we are totally dependent and cannot survive without the tender care of our Good Shepherd, Jesus Christ.

11. **Sheep are the same everywhere.** You can travel the world and find sheep being raised in a number of different countries. But whether they are in America, Russia, Israel, Turkey, Central Asia, or elsewhere, they are the same everywhere. They all have the same characteristics and behaviors. Likewise, as God's sheep, we share very similar qualities and conducts. Even many of our struggles are the same. Through it all, the Lord is our Shepherd.

As Your Good Shepherd, The Lord Promises Supernatural Provision

The first of the ten promises found in the Twenty-Third Psalm is that God is our *supernatural Provider*. David declared, "The Lord is my shepherd; I shall not want" (Psalm 23:1). Notice David didn't say, "They Lord is *their* shepherd," or "The Lord is *our* shepherd." He personalized it and said, "The Lord is *my* shepherd…." It would be good and wise for you to personalize this promise and begin declaring the same thing out of *your* mouth: "The Lord is *my* shepherd; I shall not want."

Jesus Himself confirmed this promise of supernatural provision in His sermon on the mount, which is recorded in Matthew's gospel. With great boldness He said,

> **Therefore I say unto you, Take no thought for your life, what ye shall eat, or what ye shall drink; nor yet for your body, what ye shall put on. Is not the life more than meat, and the body than raiment?**

> Behold the fowls of the air: for they sow not, neither do they reap, nor gather into barns; yet your heavenly Father feedeth them. Are ye not much better than they?
>
> Which of you by taking thought can add one cubit unto his stature?
>
> And why take ye thought for raiment? Consider the lilies of the field, how they grow; they toil not, neither do they spin:
>
> And yet I say unto you, that even Solomon in all his glory was not arrayed like one of these.
>
> Wherefore, if God so clothe the grass of the field, which to day is, and to morrow is cast into the oven, shall he not much more clothe you, O ye of little faith?
>
> Therefore take no thought, saying, What shall we eat? or, What shall we drink? or, Wherewithal shall we be clothed?
>
> (For after all these things do the Gentiles seek:) for your heavenly Father knoweth that ye have need of all these things.
>
> But seek ye first the kingdom of God, and his righteousness; and all these things shall be added unto you.
>
> — Matthew 6:25-33

Jesus made it clear that God — our heavenly Father — is going to provide all our physical needs, and we shouldn't worry about any of them. These words from the lips of Christ agree with David's declaration, "The Lord is my shepherd; I shall not want" (Psalm 23:1). The phrase "I shall not want" carries the idea of not lacking anything. God has clearly articulated it is His will to be our Ultimate Provider!

David recognized this elsewhere in his writings. Speaking from personal observation and experience in his life, he declared, "I have been young, and now am old; yet I have not seen the righteous forsaken, nor his seed [descendants] begging bread" (Psalm 37:25).

Moses made a similar declaration to the children of Israel as they were concluding their 40-year journey through the wilderness. He stated, "The Lord your God has blessed you in everything you have done. He has watched your every step through this great wilderness. During these forty years, the Lord your God has been with you, and you have lacked nothing"

(Deuteronomy 2:7 *NLT*). Friend, if God could provide for the Israelites for 40 years in the desert, He can certainly take care of us.

Again and again, He reminds us of His willingness and ability to give us what we need, when we need it. Psalm 84:11 in the *New King James* says, "For the Lord God is a sun and shield; the Lord will give grace and glory; No good thing will He withhold from those who walk uprightly." What a comfort to know that God loves, cares, and provides for us!

One little girl was trying to quote the Twenty-Third Psalm, and she inadvertently said, *"The Lord is my Shepherd, that's all I want."* Amazingly, her misquote turned out to be true! If the Lord is your Shepherd, you really do have all that you could ever want.

God Will Supply All Your Needs!

Undoubtedly, all of us go through hard times, and David was no exception. Yet out of a heart of gratefulness for all that God had done, David employed some healthy self-talk during seasons of trouble, reminding himself of the Lord's goodness in his life. He said, "Bless the Lord, O my soul, and forget not all his benefits: who forgiveth all thine iniquities; who healeth all thy diseases; who redeemeth thy life from destruction; who crowneth thee with lovingkindness and tender mercies; who satisfieth thy mouth with good things; so that thy youth is renewed like the eagle's" (Psalm 103:2-5).

Friend, if you are a born-again child of God, you have been given extraordinary benefits through Jesus Christ. He forgives *all* your sins, and He heals *all* your diseases. He has rescued you out of Satan's slave market of abuse and poured out lovingkindness and mercy on your life. On top of that, He is ready, willing, and able to provide the material blessings you need to strengthen and empower you. He is your Ultimate Provider!

The apostle Paul spoke this promise to the believers at the church in Philippi who had sacrificially supported his ministry with their financial gifts. He said, "But my God shall supply all your need according to His riches in glory by Christ Jesus" (Philippians 4:19).

Taking the original meaning of the Greek words in this verse, here is the *Renner Interpretive Version (RIV)* of Philippians 4:19:

> **But my God will supply your needs so completely that He will eliminate all your deficiencies. He will meet all your physical**

and tangible needs until you are so full that you have no more capacity to hold anything else. **He will supply all your needs until you are totally filled, packed full and overflowing to the point of bursting at the seams and spilling over!**

If you are a giver, you, too, can claim the promise in this verse. And if you are God's child, He is your Shepherd. The Lord is watching over you and He will provide for all your needs. In our next lesson, we will focus on the second promise of Psalm 23: God's Supernatural Protection.

STUDY QUESTIONS

Study to shew thyself approved unto God, a workman that needeth not to be ashamed, rightly dividing the word of truth.
— 2 Timothy 2:15

1. Did you know that God is fully aware of everything about you? It's true! Look up what the Bible says in these verses and identify the details of your life of which God is mindful.
   - Psalm 139:1-6
   - Psalm 56:8
   - Luke 12:7

   Also consider Hebrews 4:13 and First John 3:20.

2. Psalm 103:5 (*AMPC*) says, "[The Lord] satisfies your mouth [your necessity and desire at your personal age and situation] with good so that your youth, renewed, is like the eagle's [strong, overcoming, soaring]!" Take a few moments to really chew on this passage. What is the Holy Spirit speaking to you personally through this promise?

3. Do you struggle with worry? Many people do. But God doesn't want you to waste another day worrying about anything. He is your shepherd who has promised to take care of all your needs. Take time to meditate on Jesus' words in Matthew 6:25-34, along with Second Corinthians 9:8 and Hebrews 13:5. How do these promises encourage you to trust God in your current situations?

PRACTICAL APPLICATION

> But be ye doers of the word, and not hearers only,
> deceiving your own selves.
> —James 1:22

1. Take a few moments and reflect on the eleven characteristics of sheep. Which of these traits can you see manifesting in your life? How does this help you see your need for God's shepherding role in your life?
2. If you had an opportunity to brag on God, what example (or examples) of Him being a good shepherd might you share with a friend to encourage them to trust the Lord for supernatural provision? In what specific ways has He miraculously come through for you?
3. What do you need God to provide for you right now at "your personal age and situation"? Pause and pray, asking Him to specifically supply what you need in this moment of your life.

LESSON 2

TOPIC

God's Supernatural Protection

SCRIPTURES

1. **Psalm 23:1-6** — The Lord is my shepherd; I shall not want. He maketh me to lie down in green pastures: he leadeth me beside the still waters. He restoreth my soul: he leadeth me in the paths of righteousness for his name's sake. Yea, though I walk through the valley of the shadow of death, I will fear no evil: for thou art with me; thy rod and thy staff they comfort me. Thou preparest a table before me in the presence of mine enemies: thou anointest my head with oil; my cup runneth over. Surely goodness and mercy shall follow me all the days of my life: and I will dwell in the house of the Lord for ever.
2. **Ezekiel 34:11-14** — For thus saith the Lord God; Behold, I, even I, will both search my sheep, and seek them out. As a shepherd seeketh out his flock in the day that he is among his sheep that are scattered; so will I seek out my sheep, and will deliver them out of all places where they have been scattered in the cloudy and dark day. And I will

bring them out from the people, and gather them from the countries, and will bring them to their own land, and feed them upon the mountains of Israel by the rivers, and in all the inhabited places of the country. I will feed them in a good pasture, and upon the high mountains of Israel shall their fold be: there shall they lie in a good fold, and in a fat pasture shall they feed upon the mountains of Israel.
3. **Acts 20:28,29** — Take heed therefore unto yourselves, and to all the flock, over the which the Holy Ghost hath made you overseers, to feed the church of God, which he hath purchased with his own blood. For I know this, that after my departing shall grievous wolves enter in among you, not sparing the flock.
4. **John 10:11** — I am the good shepherd: the good shepherd giveth his life for the sheep.
5. **1 Peter 2:25** — For ye were as sheep going astray; but are now returned unto the Shepherd and Bishop of your souls.

GREEK WORDS

1. "for" — ὑπὲρ (*huper*): on behalf of
2. "sheep" — προβάτων (*probaton*): a flock of sheep
3. "life" — ψυχή (*psuche*): the mind, the will, and the emotions; where we get the words psyche and psychology
4. "souls" — ψυχή (*psuche*): the mind, the will, and the emotions; where we get the words psyche and psychology

SYNOPSIS

In Lesson 1, we began our study on Psalm 23, focusing on verse 1 in which David said, "The Lord is my shepherd; I shall not want." Here we see that the Lord is our Shepherd, and we are His sheep that are totally dependent on His continual loving care in our lives. God's first promise to us in this psalm is supernatural provision — it is His guarantee to supply all of our needs, a promise that appears in many places throughout Scripture. With the Lord as our Shepherd, we have everything we need!

The emphasis of this lesson:

The second promise God gives us in Psalm 23 is His supernatural protection. As we humbly submit to Jesus and allow Him to be our

Good Shepherd, He will put an end to fear, enabling us to lie down and experience rest in our souls.

The metaphor of the Lord being our Shepherd is seen in many places in the Bible. John called Jesus the *Good Shepherd* (John 10:11). Peter referred to Him as the *Chief Shepherd* (1 Peter 5:4), and the writer of Hebrews called Christ the *Great Shepherd*. More than likely, all these titles were birthed out of David's classic comparison in Psalm 23, where he wrote:

> **The Lord is my shepherd; I shall not want. He maketh me to lie down in green pastures: he leadeth me beside the still waters. He restoreth my soul: he leadeth me in the paths of righteousness for his name's sake. Yea, though I walk through the valley of the shadow of death, I will fear no evil: for thou art with me; thy rod and thy staff they comfort me. Thou preparest a table before me in the presence of mine enemies: thou anointest my head with oil; my cup runneth over. Surely goodness and mercy shall follow me all the days of my life: and I will dwell in the house of the Lord for ever.**
>
> **— Psalm 23:1-6**

In this treasured psalm, we are given ten amazing promises from the Lord. These include:

1. God's supernatural provision (Psalm 23:1)
2. God's supernatural protection (Psalm 23:2)
3. God's supernatural peace (Psalm 23:2)
4. God's supernatural restoration (Psalm 23:3)
5. God's Supernatural guidance (Psalm 23:3)
6. God's supernatural confidence (Psalm 23:4)
7. God's supernatural correction (Psalm 23:4)
8. God's supernatural prosperity (Psalm 23:5)
9. God's supernatural anointing/blessing (Psalm 23:5)
10. God's supernatural promise (Psalm 23:6)

Even if Others Fail Us, God Himself Will Shepherd Us

The second promise God makes to us as our Shepherd is found in Psalm 23:2, which says, "He maketh me to lie down in green pastures…." This verse is about God's *supernatural protection* in our lives. In addition to providing all our needs, the Lord has also vowed to be our Guardian God who never sleeps or slumbers. Psalm 121:5 and 6 in *The Message* says, "God's your Guardian, right at your side to protect you — Shielding you from sunstroke, sheltering you from moonstroke."

Interestingly, in Old Testament times, God had raised up individuals among His chosen people to serve as shepherds over Israel. Although there were many who faithfully carried out their duties, during Ezekiel's day, the majority of the shepherds of Israel had failed to fulfill their responsibilities, and God was quite upset about it. We find His response to their inaction in Ezekiel 34:11-14:

> **For thus saith the Lord God; Behold, I, even I, will both search my sheep, and seek them out. As a shepherd seeketh out his flock in the day that he is among his sheep that are scattered; so will I seek out my sheep, and will deliver them out of all places where they have been scattered in the cloudy and dark day. And I will bring them out from the people, and gather them from the countries, and will bring them to their own land, and feed them upon the mountains of Israel by the rivers, and in all the inhabited places of the country. I will feed them in a good pasture, and upon the high mountains of Israel shall their fold be: there shall they lie in a good fold, and in a fat pasture shall they feed upon the mountains of Israel.**

Basically, God told the shepherds of Israel, "If you're not going to do the job I called you to do, I Myself will step in and do it!" When all others fail in their responsibilities, God will not! He Himself will shepherd us, and His protection will enable us to "lie down in a good fold."

When Do Sheep Lie Down?

In order to fully appreciate the gift of being able to lie down, you need to understand something about sheep: They are easily frightened and thrown into a state of panic. Consequently, they run from what frightens them and band together in large groups for protection. Sheep feel safe in great numbers because it's harder for a predator to attack and snag one of them out of a group than to go after a few strays. Staying together in a pack is the only protection they have from predators — unless they have a shepherd watching over them and protecting them from harm.

Essentially, sheep will only lie down when four conditions are met:

Number 1: Sheep must be free from all fear.

Sheep are easily excited and frightened even by non-threatening activities happening around them. The only time sheep will lie down is when they are free from fear. They refuse to lie down when they're afraid.

Number 2: Sheep must be free from panicky situations.

Sheep are so easily panicked that if a jackrabbit suddenly jumps out from behind a bush, it can cause a whole flock to stampede recklessly into danger. When one startled sheep runs in fright, a dozen others will bolt with it in blind fear, not even knowing what they're running from.

Number 3: Sheep must be free from the fearful torment of flies or parasites.

Sheep will not lie down when they are tormented by flies or parasites. If parasites are present or flies are buzzing around their heads and biting their necks and backs, they will not lie down. Only when sheep are free from the fear of annoying pests will they relax.

Number 4: Sheep must be free from the fear of no food and hunger.

Sheep will only lie down when they are free from the fear of hunger. If they are afraid that they don't have enough food, they will anxiously roam about searching for sustenance to satisfy their appetite. For sheep to lie down, they must be free from the fear of hunger.

Thus, to lie down and rest, sheep must feel they are protected from every type of fear.

Believers Battle Fear Just Like Sheep

As believers, we all are just like sheep, which means we, too, are easily frightened. The Bible says fear has torment (*see* 1 John 4:18). Just living in this present age, you probably know from firsthand experience what it feels like to be tormented by fearful thoughts and feelings from the enemy.

Maybe you've been afraid of what might happen to you in the midst of this chaotic, unpredictable world that seems to be spinning out of control. Or you've been terrified of running out of money to pay your bills or running out of food to feed your family. Maybe you've been worried you would not be able to buy clothes or that you would get fired from your job due to downsizing. *What are people going to say about me?* you've agonized. *What kind of rumors are they going to spread?* Whatever fear you may be facing, it has torment with it, and it is very hard to lie down and rest when your mind is buzzing with harassing thoughts of dread and terror.

Although most fears are illogical, they can produce great insecurities and cause real inward panic that makes it impossible for us to rest. The truth is, the majority of the things we fear will *never* take place. As a part of God's flock, He promises to supernaturally protect us from all harm. His presence gives us such a sense of security that we can lie down and rest and not be fearful of some potential disaster looming ahead.

In addition to God's supernatural presence abiding with us, He has also given us — His Church — shepherds to help protect us and watch over our souls. The apostle Paul addressed the shepherds of the church in Ephesus at the time of his departure saying, "Take heed therefore unto yourselves, and to all the flock, over the which the Holy Ghost hath made you overseers, to feed the church of God, which he hath purchased with his own blood. For I know this, that after my departing shall grievous wolves enter in among you, not sparing the flock" (Acts 20:28,29).

The only way the "flock" of God's people was going to remain safe was if the shepherds in Ephesus took their positions seriously. Likewise, pastors today need to be responsible and actively watch over the people they have been entrusted by the Holy Spirit to shepherd. Nevertheless, even if your pastor neglects his protective care of you, God will not.

Jesus Is Your Good Shepherd!

In John 10:11, Jesus said, "I am the good shepherd: the good shepherd giveth his life for the sheep." What's interesting about this verse is that in the original Greek text, it quotes Jesus as saying, "I am the shepherd, the good one…." This was the equivalent of Him saying, "I am the Shepherd of all shepherds."

When Jesus said, "…The good shepherd giveth his life for the sheep" (John 10:11), the word "for" here is the Greek word *huper*, which means *on behalf of*. It carries the idea of *completeness*, signifying that Jesus gave, invested, or laid down his life *on behalf of* us, holding nothing back. The word "sheep" in Greek is the word *probaton*, and it describes *a flock of sheep*, which is what we are. Jesus was — and *is* — the supreme Shepherd who went so far as to give His own life for us, His sheep.

Interestingly, the word "life" is the Greek word *psuche*, which is the term for *the mind, the will, and the emotions*. It's where we get the words *psyche* and *psychology*. Normally, you would think that the word for "life" used here would have been the Greek word *bios*, which describes one's *physical life*, or the word *zoe*, signifying the *abundant life* that only God can give. Instead, the Holy Spirit prompted the use of the word *psuche*, which tells us that Jesus gave His mind, His will, and His emotions in His shepherding care for us!

This is a picture of **total involvement**. Jesus ultimately gave His life for us. Of His own free will, He laid His life down and surrendered to the will of the Father. He paid the highest price to care for us — purchasing our freedom with His own life's blood! Still today, Jesus remains actively involved in watching over our lives. Ultimately, it is the reassuring presence and love of Jesus that puts an end to fear.

The apostle Peter said, "For ye were as sheep going astray; but are now returned unto the Shepherd and Bishop of your souls" (1 Peter 2:25). Here again we see the Greek word *psuche*, translated here as "souls." It pinpoints the place where we battle fear — in the imaginations of our mind and the feelings of our emotions. This verse lets us know that if we will humble ourselves and submit to Jesus, and allow Him to be the Shepherd of our souls, He will put an end to fear, enabling us to lie down and rest mentally, emotionally, and physically.

Friend, the Lord is your Shepherd who makes you lie down in green pastures. You can rest in His protective care — free from all fear. In our next lesson, we will explore God's promise of supernatural peace.

STUDY QUESTIONS

**Study to shew thyself approved unto God, a workman that needeth not to be ashamed, rightly dividing the word of truth.
— 2 Timothy 2:15**

1. Carefully reflect on God's words in Ezekiel 34:11-14. Of all the beautiful ways God promises to protect us in these verses, what aspect of His care do you most appreciate? Why is this so important to you?

2. Jesus told us He is the Good Shepherd who gives His life on behalf of us, His sheep (*see* John 10:11). What other amazing things did Jesus come to do? (Consider Isaiah 61:1-3; Luke 4:18; John 10:10; and 1 John 3:8.)

3. In addition to setting you free from the power of sin (*see* Romans 6:6-8,18,22) and removing you from the kingdom of darkness and placing you into the kingdom of light (*see* Colossians 1:13), what does Hebrews 7:23-25 say Jesus is doing for you today and every day of your life?

PRACTICAL APPLICATION

> But be ye doers of the word, and not hearers only,
> deceiving your own selves.
> —James 1:22

1. Like sheep, we can be easily frightened and become deeply worried over circumstances and situations to the point that we are unable to rest. What fears are weighing most heavily on your mind and emotions right now?

2. If you've ever been mistreated or neglected by a leader, you know the pain it causes and how it can usher you into a level of fear and distrust of other leaders — often without even thinking. How does knowing that Jesus gave His all for you — body, soul, and spirit — encourage you to trust Him and entrust yourself to the care of the leaders He's placed over you? Do you believe He really has your best interest at heart? If not, pray and ask the Holy Spirit to show you why.

LESSON 3

TOPIC

God's Supernatural Peace

SCRIPTURES

1. **Psalm 23:1-6** — The Lord is my shepherd; I shall not want. He maketh me to lie down in green pastures: he leadeth me beside the still waters. He restoreth my soul: he leadeth me in the paths of righteousness for his name's sake. Yea, though I walk through the valley of

the shadow of death, I will fear no evil: for thou art with me; thy rod and thy staff they comfort me. Thou preparest a table before me in the presence of mine enemies: thou anointest my head with oil; my cup runneth over. Surely goodness and mercy shall follow me all the days of my life: and I will dwell in the house of the Lord for ever.

2. **John 14:1,27** (*NKJV*) — Let not your heart be troubled; you believe in God, believe also in Me.... Peace I leave with you, My peace I give to you; not as the world gives do I give to you. Let not your heart be troubled, neither let it be afraid.
3. **2 Timothy 1:6,7** — Wherefore I put thee in remembrance that thou stir up the gift of God, which is in thee by the putting on of my hands. For God hath not given us the spirit of fear; but of power, and of love, and of a sound mind.
4. **Isaiah 26:3** — Thou wilt keep him in perfect peace, whose mind is stayed on thee: because he trusteth in thee.
5. **Isaiah 26:3** (*TPT*) — Perfect, absolute peace surrounds those whose imaginations are consumed with you; they confidently trust in you.
6. **1 Samuel 30:6** (*AMPC*) — David was greatly distressed... But David encouraged and strengthened himself in the Lord his God.
7. **Psalm 94:19** (*NIV*) — When anxiety was great within me, your consolation brought me joy.

GREEK WORDS

1. "troubled" — ταράσσω (*tarasso*): to shake, to trouble, to disquiet, to unsettle, to perplex, to cause anxiety, or even to cause feelings of grief; it is the picture of one who feels inwardly shaken, unsettled, confused, and upset
2. "peace" — εἰρήνη (*eirene*): the cessation of war; conflict put away; a time of rebuilding and reconstruction after war has ceased; distractions removed; a time of prosperity; the rule of order in the place of chaos; it is a calm, inner stability that results in the ability to conduct oneself peacefully even in the midst of circumstances that would normally be traumatic or upsetting; it is the Greek equivalent for the Hebrew word "shalom," which expresses the idea of wholeness, completeness, or tranquility in the soul that is unaffected by outward circumstances or pressures

3. "leave" — ἀφίημι (*aphiemi*): to permanently release; to impart; to set free; to let go; complete liberation
4. "heart" — καρδία (*kardia*): the heart; although this word was sometimes used to denote the heart as a physical organ, it was regularly employed throughout the Old Testament, Classical Greek literature, and the New Testament to describe the inner self, spirit, or center of a person; it involves the elements of emotion, instinct, and passion
5. "afraid" — δειλός (*deilos*): a gripping fear or dread that produces a shrinking back or cowardice; a dread that saps one's ability to look at a problem head-on and causes him to retreat; to be timid or a coward
6. "spirit" — πνεῦμα (*pneuma*): spirit, like a spiritual force
7. "fear" — δειλός (*deilos*): a gripping fear or dread that produces a shrinking back or cowardice; a dread that saps one's ability to look at a problem head-on and causes him to retreat; to be timid or a coward
8. "power" — δύναμις (*dunamis*): power; it carries the idea of explosive, superhuman power that comes with enormous energy and produces phenomenal, extraordinary, and unparalleled results; depicts miraculous powers that are impressive, incomparable, and beyond human ability to perform
9. "love" — ἀγάπη (*agape*): a divine love that gives and gives, even if it's never responded to, thanked, or acknowledged; a love so profound that it knows no limits or boundaries in how far, wide, high, and deep it will go to show that love to its recipient; a self-sacrificial love that moves the lover to action
10. "sound mind" — σωφρονισμός (*sophronismos*): sound mind; reasonable; balanced; levelheaded in the way one thinks; to think clearly about oneself or a situation; a saved or delivered mind

SYNOPSIS

In our last lesson, we explored the meaning of the first half of Psalm 23:2, where David said, "He maketh me to lie down in green pastures...." This verse tells us that when we allow the Lord to shepherd our lives, His presence gives us such a sense of security that we can lie down and rest, living free of all tormenting fears that come against our mind, will, and emotions. What a priceless blessing!

The emphasis of this lesson:

In addition to the Lord's promise of supernatural provision and protection, He also guarantees us His supernatural peace — a priceless tranquility in our soul that is unaffected by outward circumstances or pressures. His peace is to be a permanent resident, providing us a calm, internal stability even in the midst of traumatic events.

A Review of Psalm 23 and God's Ten Guarantees

Before becoming the king of Israel, David spent a number of his young adult years as a shepherd to his father's sheep. As he grew in his relationship with the Lord, he wrote many psalms. One of these is Psalm 23, where he compared the Lord's tender care of us with that of a shepherd. He declared:

> The Lord is my shepherd; I shall not want. He maketh me to lie down in green pastures: he leadeth me beside the still waters. He restoreth my soul: he leadeth me in the paths of righteousness for his name's sake. Yea, though I walk through the valley of the shadow of death, I will fear no evil: for thou art with me; thy rod and thy staff they comfort me. Thou preparest a table before me in the presence of mine enemies: thou anointest my head with oil; my cup runneth over. Surely goodness and mercy shall follow me all the days of my life: and I will dwell in the house of the Lord for ever.
> — Psalm 23:1-6

Here in these six verses, God makes ten guarantees to you and all those who surrender their lives to Him and allow Him to be their shepherd. God promises...

1. **Supernatural provision (Psalm 23:1)**
2. **Supernatural protection (Psalm 23:2)**
3. **Supernatural peace (Psalm 23:2)**
4. **Supernatural restoration (Psalm 23:3)**
5. **Supernatural guidance (Psalm 23:3)**
6. **Supernatural confidence (Psalm 23:4)**
7. **Supernatural correction (Psalm 23:4)**
8. **Supernatural prosperity (Psalm 23:5)**

9. **Supernatural anointing/blessing (Psalm 23:5)**
10. **Supernatural promise (Psalm 23:6)**

After telling us about God's supernatural protection, David went on to say that the Lord leads us "…beside the still waters" (Psalm 23:2). The words "still waters" paint a picture of *serenity, tranquility*, and *peace* that God promises His people. In a world filled with agitation and turmoil, we should always be mindful of that empowering sense of calm and security that only comes from Jesus.

As renowned author C. S. Lewis so eloquently stated, "God cannot give us happiness and peace apart from Himself, because… there is no such thing." Indeed, Isaiah called Jesus "the Prince of Peace" (*see* Isaiah 9:6), and if we will come to Him — especially in the midst of the most overwhelming circumstances — He will impart His supernatural peace to our hearts and minds. All we need to do is ask.

What Did Jesus Say About Peace?

Just hours before being scourged with Roman whips and crucified on the Cross, Jesus spent His final moments speaking words of wisdom and encouragement to His closest friends. Knowing what was about to happen and the aftermath of grief and confusion that would ensue, Jesus turned to His disciples and said:

> **Let not your heart be troubled; you believe in God, believe also in Me. Peace I leave with you, My peace I give to you; not as the world gives do I give to you. Let not your heart be troubled, neither let it be afraid.**
>
> **John 14:1,27 (*NKJV*)**

Twice Jesus urged His followers, "Let not your heart be troubled…." The word "troubled" here is the Greek word *tarasso*, which means *to shake, to trouble, to disquiet, to unsettle, to perplex, to cause anxiety,* or even *to cause feelings of grief.* It is the picture of one who feels inwardly shaken, unsettled, confused, and upset. By using this word *tarasso* — translated here as "troubled" — Jesus was literally telling us, "Don't let your heart be shaken, troubled, unsettled, anxious, or filled with feelings of grief."

Why? Because Jesus said, "*Peace* I leave with you, My *peace* I give to you…" (John 14:2 *NKJV*). The meaning of the word "peace" is extremely important. It is the Greek word *eirene*, and it is used throughout the New

Testament to describe *the peace of God*. This word was first used to depict *the cessation of war or conflict put away*. It pictures a time of rebuilding and reconstruction after war has ceased. The distractions have been removed, and a time of prosperity has set in. The rule of order has taken the place of chaos.

Furthermore, this word *eirene* — the word for "peace" — *describes a calm, inner stability* that results in the ability to conduct oneself peacefully even in the midst of circumstances that would normally be traumatic or upsetting. It is actually the Greek equivalent for the Hebrew word "shalom," which expresses the idea of *wholeness, completeness* or *tranquility in the soul* that is unaffected by outward circumstances or pressures.

God's Peace Is To Become a Permanent Resident in Your Heart

So when Jesus says He has given us His "peace," He is basically saying, "The conflicts and warlike disturbances that were once active in your soul have been removed. I have established a cease fire and brought about a calm, inner stability and tranquility in your mind, will, and emotions. Peace has come in the place of chaos. It is time to rebuild."

Jesus said, "Peace I leave with you…." The word "leave" here is the Greek word *aphiemi*, and it means *to permanently release; to impart; to set free*; or *to let go*. It is a picture of *complete liberation*. Thus, when Jesus said, "Peace I leave with you," it was the equivalent of Him saying, "I'm permanently releasing my peace to you, and I want it to stay with you for the rest of your life."

Where does Jesus want His peace to take up residence? In your *heart*. He said, "…Let not your heart be troubled, neither let it be afraid" (John 14:27 *NKJV*). The word "heart" is the Greek word *kardia*, which describes *the heart* and it's where we get the words *cardiac* and *cardiac arrest*.

Although this word was sometimes used to denote the heart as a physical organ, it was regularly employed throughout the Old Testament, Classical Greek literature, and the New Testament to describe *the inner self*, *spirit*, or *center of a person*. It involves the elements of emotion, instinct, and passion.

Therefore, when Jesus says, "Peace I leave with you, My peace I give to you. Let not your heart be troubled," He is essentially saying, "Don't let your inner self — the core of who you are — be shaken, troubled, unsettled, or anxious by the things you see and hear around you. I have permanently given you My supernatural peace to calm you and provide an internal stability even in the midst of traumatic events."

Fear Is a Spiritual Force

Not only does Jesus want your heart free from trouble, He also doesn't want you to be *afraid*. This word "afraid" used in John 14:27 is the Greek word *deilos*, and it depicts *a gripping fear or dread that produces a shrinking back or cowardice*. It is a dread that saps one's ability to look at a problem head-on and causes him to retreat. It means to be timid or a coward.

The apostle Paul used this same Greek word — the word *deilos* — in his instruction to his young apprentice Timothy. Knowing the difficulties Timothy was facing, Paul said, "Wherefore I put thee in remembrance that thou stir up the gift of God, which is in thee by the putting on of my hands. For God hath not given us the spirit of fear; but of power, and of love, and of a sound mind" (2 Timothy 1:6,7).

Let's look at verse 7 once more and insert the word "shepherd" for God. It says, "For God — our *Shepherd* — hath not given us the spirit of fear; but of power, and of love, and of a sound mind." First of all, we see that *fear is a spirit*. The word "spirit" in this verse is the Greek word *pneuma*, and it denotes a *spirit*, like *a spiritual force*. Fear is a spiritual force that comes against us to stop us from moving forward into what God has instructed us to do.

Also notice the word "fear" in Second Timothy 1:7. It is once again the Greek word *deilos*, the same word Jesus used in John 14:27, which is translated as "afraid." It describes *a gripping fear or dread that produces a shrinking back or cowardice*; a dread that saps one's ability to look at a problem head-on and causes him to retreat.

We've Been Given a Spirit of 'Power, Love, and a Sound Mind'

Rather than give us a spirit of fear, our Shepherd has given us His own Spirit — one of "...power, and of love, and of a sound mind" (2 Timothy 1:7). The word "power" is a form of the Greek word *dunamis*, which means *power* and carries the idea of *explosive, superhuman power that comes with enormous energy and produces phenomenal, extraordinary, and unparalleled results*. This word depicts miraculous powers that are impressive, incomparable, and beyond human ability to perform.

God's Spirit is also one of "love." In Greek, the word "love" is *agape*, and it denotes *a divine love that gives and gives, even if it's never responded to, thanked, or acknowledged*. This love is so profound that it knows no limits or boundaries in how far, wide, high, and deep it will go to show that love to its recipient. It is a self-sacrificial love that moves the lover to action. So not only has God deposited His explosive, superhuman power in you, but also His supernatural love.

Furthermore, the Bible goes on to say that our Shepherd has also given us a "sound mind." This phrase is a translation of the Greek word *sophronismos*, which is a compound of the word *sodzo*, meaning *salvation* or *deliverance*, and the word *phroneo*, the root for the word *mind*. When these two words are put together, it is translated as *sound mind*, and it describes *one that is reasonable, balanced, and levelheaded in the way he thinks*; *one who thinks clearly about himself or a situation*. Essentially, a "sound mind" — the word *sophronismos* — pictures a *saved brain* or *delivered mind*, which is quite the opposite of a mind paralyzed by fear, panic, and illogical thinking. Thus, God has rescued and salvaged your mind, giving you the ability to think clearly and accurately and not be driven by a spirit of fear! Praise His mighty Name!

What You Think About Is the Key To Experiencing Peace

The prophet Isaiah really spells out the connection between the thoughts of our mind and having God's peace. He said, "Thou wilt keep him in perfect peace, whose mind is stayed on thee: because he trusteth in thee" (Isaiah 26:3). *The Passion Translation* of this verse says, "Perfect, absolute peace surrounds those whose imaginations are consumed with you; they confidently trust in you."

This scripture leads us to a very important question each of us needs to ask ourselves on a regular basis: *What am I thinking about? What kinds of thoughts are consuming my mind?* The fact is, anxious thoughts will always present themselves, but *still waters* are available as we turn our focus on Jesus and allow Him to release His peace into our hearts and minds.

David learned how to follow the Lord, his Shepherd, and come to the peaceful place of still waters. First Samuel 30:6 (*AMPC*) says, "David was greatly distressed... But David encouraged and strengthened himself in the Lord his God." And Psalm 94:19 in the *New International Version* says, "When anxiety was great within me, your consolation brought me joy."

Friend, the Lord is your Shepherd, and as you come to Him and fix your focus on the promises of His Word and remember His faithful track record throughout your life, you, too, will receive His peace and be comforted within by His Spirit. In our next lesson, we will discover what David meant when he said that the Lord "restores our soul."

STUDY QUESTIONS

> Study to shew thyself approved unto God, a workman that needeth not to be ashamed, rightly dividing the word of truth.
> — 2 Timothy 2:15

1. What is "the peace of God" and how do we access it? God answers this question through the writings of the apostle Paul in Philippians 4:6-8 (*TLB*):

    "Don't worry about anything; instead, pray about everything; tell God your needs and don't forget to thank him for his answers. If you do this, you will experience God's peace, which is far more wonderful than the human mind can understand. His peace will keep your thoughts and your hearts quiet and at rest as you trust in Christ Jesus. ...Fix your thoughts on what is true and good and right. Think about things that are pure and lovely, and dwell on the fine, good things in others. Think about all you can praise God for and be glad about."

    According to this passage, what actions does God say *you* need to take — *regularly* — in order to receive and experience His supernatural peace?

2. Jesus said, "Peace I leave with you, my peace I give unto you... (John 14:27), and the meaning of this word "peace" is a time when war is over and things are calm enough to rebuild. Friend, Jesus has already won the war! And He wants you to begin seeing and living your life from the place of victory He has paid for with His own blood. Take a look at these verses and identify the things over which He has already given you victory.

- John 16:33
- Colossians 2:15
- Romans 8:35,37
- 1 John 5:4,5
- 2 Corinthians 2:14

PRACTICAL APPLICATION

> But be ye doers of the word, and not hearers only, deceiving your own selves.
> —James 1:22

1. Do you find yourself anxious or overwhelmed by life? Stop and ask yourself, *What kind of things am I thinking about? On what is my mind focused?* Take some time to journal and pray about what is on your mind and receive Jesus' peace.
2. What situations or circumstances are you facing right now that are sapping you of strength and stealing your peace? What are you afraid of? If you're not sure, pray and ask the Holy Spirit to reveal it to you. Then surrender it to God and ask Him to deliver you from all fears (*see* Psalm 34:4).
3. First Samuel 30:6 says that when David was greatly distressed, he "…encouraged and strengthened himself in the Lord his God." What aspects of God's care of you in Psalm 23 can you remind yourself of that will encourage you when you're distressed and anxious?

LESSON 4

TOPIC

God's Supernatural Restoration

SCRIPTURES

1. **Psalm 23:1-6** — The Lord is my shepherd; I shall not want. He maketh me to lie down in green pastures: he leadeth me beside the still waters. He restoreth my soul: he leadeth me in the paths of righ-

teousness for his name's sake. Yea, though I walk through the valley of the shadow of death, I will fear no evil: for thou art with me; thy rod and thy staff they comfort me. Thou preparest a table before me in the presence of mine enemies: thou anointest my head with oil; my cup runneth over. Surely goodness and mercy shall follow me all the days of my life: and I will dwell in the house of the Lord for ever.

2. **Jeremiah 30:17** — For I will restore health to you and heal you of your wounds, says the Lord....
3. **John 10:10** — The thief cometh not, but for to steal, and to kill, and to destroy: I am come that they might have life, and that they might have it more abundantly.
4. **Luke 19:10** — For the Son of man is come to seek and to save that which was lost.
5. **Isaiah 57:15** (*NLT*) — The high and lofty one who lives in eternity, the Holy One, says this: 'I live in the high and holy place with those whose spirits are contrite and humble. I restore the crushed spirit of the humble and revive the courage of those with repentant hearts.'
6. **Luke 4:18,19** — The Spirit of the Lord is upon me, because he hath anointed me to preach the gospel to the poor; he hath sent me to heal the brokenhearted, to preach deliverance to the captives, and recovering of sight to the blind, to set at liberty them that are bruised, to preach the acceptable year of the Lord.

GREEK WORDS

1. "lost" — ἀπολωλός (*apololos*): derived from the word *apollumi*, and it conveys the idea of something ruined, wasted, trashed, devastated, or destroyed; the same word for the Destroyer — one of the New Testament names to describe Satan's demented nature
2. "seek" — ζητέω (*zeteo*): to desire, to pursue, seek, or earnestly search for; a person so intent on achieving his goal that he will search, seek, and investigate, never giving up in his pursuit to get what he wants
3. "save" — σῴζω (*sodzo*): implies rescue, such as a rescue from a raging sea, rescue from an illness, rescue from immediate danger; inherent in this type of "rescue" is one's return to safety and soundness
4. "brokenhearted" — συντρίβω (*suntribo*): used to describe the crushing of grapes with the feet, or the smashing and grinding of bones into dust; depicts people who have been walked on by others, those

who have been crushed by others, or those who feel they have been smashed to pieces by life or relationships

5. "heal" — ἰάομαι (*iaomai*): to cure; usually refers to a progressive cure; often depicts a healing power that progressively reverses a condition over a period of time, or a sickness that is progressively healed rather than instantaneously healed

6. "deliverance" — ἄφεσις (*aphesis*): a release; a dismissal; to set free; to permanently loose

7. "captives" — αἰχμάλωτος (*aichmalotos*): captives; those taken captive at the point of a spear; those who are dragged into bondage; manipulated by bondage

8. "recovering of sight" — ἀνάβλεψις (*anablepsis*): the returning of one's sight; the restoration of sight; to see again

9. "blind" — τυφλός (*tuphlos*): blind; it doesn't just depict a person who is unable to see, but a person who has been intentionally blinded by someone else; can picture one whose eyes have been deliberately removed so that he is blinded; that individual hasn't just lost his sight, but he has no eyes with which to see

10. "set at liberty" — ἄφεσις (*aphesis*) a release; a dismissal; to permanently loose; to set free; in this case, from the detrimental effects of a shattered life; the Greek speaks of a permanent release from the destructive effects of brokenness

11. "bruised" — τεθραυσμένους (*tethrausmenous*): to crush; to break down; depicts a person who has been shattered or fractured by life; pictures those whose lives have been continually split up and fragmented

SYNOPSIS

In our first three lessons, we have seen that the Lord is our loving Shepherd who supernaturally supplies all of our needs and maintains a protective covering over us at all times. He also provides us with an unshakable peace that calms our hearts and minds even in the midst of difficult and unpredictable circumstances. It's no wonder David urged us to "Give unto the Lord the glory due his name; worship the Lord in the beauty of holiness" (Psalm 29:2) Indeed, there is truly no one like the Lord!

The emphasis of this lesson:

As our Good Shepherd, the Lord also promises to restore our soul. His restoration is a full-scale rescue operation that results in total redemption and wholeness in Him.

An Accurate Illustration of a Good Shepherd

Just as there are good mechanics and bad mechanics, good doctors and bad doctors, there are also good shepherds and bad shepherds. David paints a vivid picture of what a good shepherd looks like in Psalm 23 — a passage that has become one of the most recognized portions of Scripture. Drawing from the pages of his personal relationship with the Lord, David said:

> The Lord is my shepherd; I shall not want. He maketh me to lie down in green pastures: he leadeth me beside the still waters. He restoreth my soul: he leadeth me in the paths of righteousness for his name's sake. Yea, though I walk through the valley of the shadow of death, I will fear no evil: for thou art with me; thy rod and thy staff they comfort me. Thou preparest a table before me in the presence of mine enemies: thou anointest my head with oil; my cup runneth over. Surely goodness and mercy shall follow me all the days of my life: and I will dwell in the house of the Lord for ever.
> — Psalm 23:1-6

Within this chapter, there are ten specific promises God makes to every person who submits to His leadership as the shepherd of their souls.

1. God promises **supernatural provision (Psalm 23:1)**.
2. God promises **supernatural protection (Psalm 23:2)**.
3. God promises **supernatural peace (Psalm 23:2)**.
4. God promises **supernatural restoration (Psalm 23:3)**.
5. God promises **supernatural guidance (Psalm 23:3)**.
6. God promises **supernatural confidence (Psalm 23:4)**.
7. God promises **supernatural correction (Psalm 23:4)**.
8. God promises **supernatural prosperity (Psalm 23:5)**.
9. God promises **supernatural anointing/blessing (Psalm 23:5)**.
10. God promises **supernatural promise (Psalm 23:6)**.

If there is one thing we can all agree on, it is that we are living in a broken world, and it can often take its toll on our lives. The truth is, all of us have experienced various hurts and pains from others. Insults, abuse, neglect, disappointments, and mistreatments of all kinds have left diverse wounds in our souls. The good news is Jesus is the restorer of souls! As our Good Shepherd, the Bible says, "He restoreth my soul…" (Psalm 23:3).

This declaration of restoration is a theme echoed in many places of Scripture, including Jeremiah 30:17 (*NKJV*), which says, "For I will restore health to you and heal you of your wounds, says the Lord.…" When life bruises and afflicts us, Jesus is ready and willing to heal and restore. It is an inseparable part of His nature.

A Picture of Real-Life Restoration

To help us have a better understanding of what it means to restore something, Rick shared a practical example of a restoration project he and his wife, Denise, undertook in their early years of living in Riga, the capital of Latvia. Their family had purchased an old apartment in a downtown building that was originally constructed in 1898. It had 13 rooms and 7 fireplaces and was an ideal living space for the Renner's growing family. At its onset, it was a very elegant building in Riga's most prestigious neighborhood. But after 55 years of communism, the whole area had become dilapidated.

You may remember the movie *Dr. Zhivago* in which the doctor returned to his home after communism came to power, and he found that his once luxurious residence had been confiscated and subdivided into multiple family dwellings. That is exactly what had taken place with the apartment the Renners were considering purchasing in Riga. At the time Rick and Denise took ownership, the ceilings were collapsing, the plastered walls were crumbling, the windows were broken out, and mold was growing everywhere. To top it off, hooligans had painted derogatory words and nasty phrases all over the walls throughout the apartment.

As unbelievable as it may seem, there were eight families living amid that horrendous mess — sharing one kitchen and one bathroom! It was shameful to see what had happened to this once-luxurious apartment where an elite class of people had formerly lived. The current occupants had no respect whatsoever for this architectural treasure. Although it was difficult to imagine, Rick was able to envision the great potential of the apartment as he and Denise initially walked through it. He saw hints of its old beauty that somehow still remained. Under 55 years of botched paint jobs, he was able to see glimpses of restored crown molding, glistening high ceilings, and lavish fireplaces so spectacular that they should be on display in a museum.

As deplorable as the apartment was, Rick and Denise knew it was for them. Although dirt, grime, filth, and trash were heaped in huge piles in every room, they knew the place could be beautiful if they would be willing to do what was necessary to bring it back to its former glory. And because of its condemned state, it was available for a low price. Once they purchased it, they immediately went to work restoring it.

Little by little, new life was infused into every crack and crevice. From the painted-over parquet floors and the mold-laden walls to the crumbling, collapsed ceilings, every facet of the apartment was worked on and overhauled. After almost a year of nonstop work, the dilapidated apartment was amazingly restored to its original glory. Because the Renners were willing to accept the challenge and restore the property, they were rewarded with something very glorious and magnificent that eventually emerged from what was once ravaged, wasted, and devastated.

Jesus Came To Restore Our Lives

When we think about the dreadful condition of the Renner's Riga apartment and all the work that was required to restore it, it is a reminder of the in-depth restoration that is needed to restore a human life. Although Satan and his imps are in the destruction business, always seeking to trash people's lives, Jesus is in the restoration business. He makes this contrast clear in John 10:10, where He says:

> **The thief cometh not, but for to steal, and to kill, and to destroy: I am come that they might have life, and that they might have it more abundantly.**

Taking into account the original Greek meaning of the text, here is the *Renner Interpretive Version (RIV)* of John 10:10:

> **The thief wants to get his hands into every good thing in your life. In fact, this pickpocket is looking for any opportunity to wiggle his way so deeply into your personal affairs that he can walk off with everything you hold precious and dear. And**

that's not all. When he's finished stealing all your goods and possessions, he'll take his plan to rob you blind to the next level by creating conditions and situations so horrible that you'll see no way to solve the problems except to sacrifice everything that remains from previous attacks. The goal of this thief is to totally devastate your life. If nothing stops him, he'll leave you insolvent, flat broke, and cleaned out in every area of your life. You'll end up feeling as if you're finished and out of business. Make no mistake. The enemy's ultimate aim is to obliterate you.

But I have specifically come with the express purpose that you will have, hold, and possess a phenomenal and amazing life. My purpose is that you will possess life so full that it overflows and spills over like a mighty river so full of water that its banks can no longer contain it all. I'm talking about an amazingly full, spirited, and vivacious life that is literally overflowing and spilling over. I have explicitly come so you can possess an abundant, profuse, plentiful, and bountiful life.

Friend, whatever Satan has tried to spoil, *Jesus has the power to restore*! Just as Rick and Denise rolled up their sleeves and began to peel back 55 years of Soviet wallpaper and paint from the walls, Jesus will go to work in you peeling back and removing the hurt and dirt of your past life one layer at a time.

His Restoration Is a Full-Scale Rescue Operation

In Luke 19:10 Jesus went on to say, "For the Son of man is come to seek and to save that which was lost." The word "lost" here has a more extensive meaning than what you might think. It is the Greek word *apololos*, which is derived from the word *apollumi*, and it conveys the idea of *something ruined, wasted, trashed, devastated, or destroyed*. It is the same word for the Destroyer — one of the New Testament names to describe Satan's demented nature. The use of this word tells us that Jesus — the Son of Man — came to seek and save that which was *ruined, wasted, trashed, devastated, or destroyed*.

The word "seek" is also significant. It is a translation of the Greek word *zeteo*, which means *to desire, to pursue, seek, or earnestly search for*. It is the picture of a person so intent on achieving his goal that he will search, seek, and investigate, never giving up in his pursuit to get what he wants. This word signifies that Jesus *has put forth* and *is putting forth* His best efforts to actively seek, save, and restore whatever Satan has tried to steal, kill, or destroy.

What does the word "save" mean? In this case, the word "save" is the Greek word *sodzo*, and it signifies *a rescue operation*, such as a rescue from a raging sea, rescue from an illness, or a rescue from immediate danger. Inherent in this type of "rescue" is one's return to safety and soundness. Thus, Jesus' work to save us isn't just a *salvage operation* — it's a full-scale *rescue* that results in a *redemptive* and *fully restorative operation*.

To be clear: When Christ finishes His work in us, we are *not* a weaker, substandard version of what we were before. On the contrary, we're stronger, better, and more improved because of what Jesus has done to *rescue* us and to *redeem* and *restore* our hearts and lives to a state of wholeness in Him! We are *not* a second-rate version of something that we used to be. In Christ, we are filled with the potential of the Holy Spirit who lives inside us.

Rick and Denise never saw the original state of the apartment that was built in Riga in 1898. But if they compare the completely restored apartment to the condition it was in when they first found it, the transformation is absolutely amazing! How could such a horrible, dilapidated place once again be beautiful and whole? To accomplish such a task required faith, imagination, hard work, and a lot of prayer. It didn't happen overnight. It was a daily effort. With hard work, faith, prayer, and the help of others, the results were breathtaking!

Likewise, Jesus is seeking to perform a rescue operation in every area of *your* life where Satan has attempted to bring devastation and ruin. He also seeks to rescue and restore those around you who need rescuing. Don't give up on them, because rescue operations are Jesus' specialty! If you will participate with Him in what He is trying to restore in your life and the lives of others, He will restore you and them, making you and those around you better than ever before!

Christ's Efforts Are Multifaceted and Far-Reaching

From the moment Jesus launched out into ministry, His mission to rescue and restore has been quite clear. This is captured vividly in Luke's gospel when He came to Nazareth and stood up in the synagogue on the Sabbath to read from the words of Isaiah. He declared:

The Spirit of the Lord is upon me, because he hath anointed me to preach the gospel to the poor; he hath sent me to heal the brokenhearted, to preach deliverance to the captives, and recovering of sight to the blind, to set at liberty them that are bruised, to preach the acceptable year of the Lord.
— **Luke 4:18,19**

There are several key words here in Jesus' mission of restoration we need to understand, including the word "brokenhearted." This is a translation of the Greek word *suntribo*, which is used to describe *the crushing of grapes with the feet*, or *the smashing and grinding of bones into dust*. In this verse, it depicts people who have been walked on or who have been crushed by others or those who feel they have been smashed to pieces by life or relationships. These are the "brokenhearted" that Jesus came to *heal*.

This word "heal" is the very unique word *iaomai*, which means *to cure* and usually refers to *a progressive cure*. It often depicts a healing power that progressively reverses a condition over a period of time, or a sickness that is progressively healed rather than instantaneously healed.

Along with healing the brokenhearted, Jesus came to "preach deliverance to the captives." The word "deliverance" is the Greek word *aphesis*, which describes *a release* or *a dismissal*. It means *to set free* or *to permanently loose*. Jesus came to permanently deliver, set free, and release the "captives." In Greek, the word "captives" is *aichmalotos*, a word used to depict *those taken captive at the point of a spear*. It is the picture of individuals who are dragged into bondage or manipulated by bondage.

Next, we see Christ's restorative work includes "recovering of sight to the blind." The phrase "recovery of sight" is a translation of the Greek word *anablepsis*, which describes *the returning of one's sight* or *the restoration of sight*. It literally means *to see again*, which means Jesus wants to restore our sight so that we can see things clearly and correctly.

This brings us to the word "blind" — the Greek word *tuphlos*, which means *blind*. What is interesting about this word is that it doesn't just depict a person who is unable to see, but *a person who has been intentionally blinded by someone else*. It can picture one whose eyes have been deliberately removed so that he is blinded. Hence, this individual hasn't just lost his sight; he has no eyes with which to see. There are many people who have become blinded in life, and Jesus wants to come and restore their sight.

Moreover, the Bible says God has anointed Jesus to "...set at liberty them that are bruised" (Luke 4:18). The words "set at liberty" are derived from the Greek word *aphesis*, the same word translated as "deliverance." It describes *a release* or *a dismissal*. It means *to permanently loose or set free*, and in this case, it means to permanently set free from the detrimental effects of a shattered life.

This ties into the meaning of the word "bruised," which is a Greek word that means *to crush* or *to break down*. It depicts a person who has been shattered or fractured by life; it is a picture of those whose lives have been continually split up and fragmented. Therefore, when Jesus said He came to "set at liberty them that are bruised," the Greek emphatically speaks of a permanent release from the destructive effects of brokenness.

Friend, if you feel brokenhearted or if you have been taken captive by some addiction, there is hope! If you feel like you've been blinded by hardships and hurts or fractured and shattered by life's disappointments and difficulties, Jesus wants to totally restore your sight and permanently release you from the destructive effects of brokenness.

In our next lesson, we will explore the fifth promise the Lord has made to us — the promise of supernatural direction found in Psalm 23:3.

STUDY QUESTIONS

> **Study to shew thyself approved unto God, a workman that needeth not to be ashamed, rightly dividing the word of truth.**
> **— 2 Timothy 2:15**

1. Take a few moments and reflect on the *Renner Interpretive Version (RIV)* of John 10:10. What is the Holy Spirit revealing to you about Satan's calculated efforts? How does this help you see where the enemy is trying to worm his way into your life? How do Jesus' words bring encouragement and hope to your soul?
2. One of the restorative works Jesus came to provide is "recovery of sight to the blind" (Luke 4:18). What does Second Corinthians 2:4 say about the people living in the world all around you — including some of your friends and loved ones? In light of Paul's words in Second Corinthians 4:6, what should you pray for these individuals? (Also consider Psalm 18:28 and 119:130; Proverbs 29:13; Isaiah 29:18.)

PRACTICAL APPLICATION

> But be ye doers of the word, and not hearers only,
> deceiving your own selves.
> —James 1:22

1. Looking back at your spiritual journey, what would you say are some of the layers of "dirt" and "dilapidation" in your past that Jesus has removed? How has His restorative work healed your hurts and improved the quality of your life?
2. Where has Satan attempted to bring devastation and ruin in your life? In what areas do you need Jesus to perform a *rescue operation*? Pray and ask Him to show you what you can begin doing right now to cooperate with His restoration in your life.

LESSON 5

TOPIC
God's Supernatural Guidance

SCRIPTURES

1. **Psalm 23:1-6** — The Lord is my shepherd; I shall not want. He maketh me to lie down in green pastures: he leadeth me beside the still waters. He restoreth my soul: he leadeth me in the paths of righteousness for his name's sake. Yea, though I walk through the valley of the shadow of death, I will fear no evil: for thou art with me; thy rod and thy staff they comfort me. Thou preparest a table before me in the presence of mine enemies: thou anointest my head with oil; my cup runneth over. Surely goodness and mercy shall follow me all the days of my life: and I will dwell in the house of the Lord for ever.
2. **Luke 4:18,19** — The Spirit of the Lord is upon me, because he hath anointed me to preach the gospel to the poor; he hath sent me to heal the brokenhearted, to preach deliverance to the captives, and recovering of sight to the blind, to set at liberty them that are bruised, to preach the acceptable year of the Lord.
3. **Psalm 32:8** (*NKJV*) — I will instruct you and teach you in the way you should go; I will guide you with My eye.

4. **Psalm 37:23** (*NLT*) — The Lord directs the steps of the godly. He delights in every detail of their lives.
5. **Psalm 73:24** (*NLT*) — You guide me with your counsel, leading me to a glorious destiny.
6. **Proverbs 3:6** (*NKJV*) — In all your ways acknowledge Him, and He shall direct your paths.
7. **Psalm 119:105** — Thy word is a lamp unto my feet, and a light unto my path.
8. **John 16:13** — Howbeit when he, the Spirit of truth, is come, he will guide you into all truth….
9. **Romans 8:14** (*NKJV*) — For as many as are led by the Spirit of God, these are sons of God.

GREEK WORDS

1. "brokenhearted" — συντρίβω (*suntribo*): used to describe the crushing of grapes with the feet, or the smashing and grinding of bones into dust; depicts people who have been walked on by others, those who have been crushed by others, or those who feel they have been smashed to pieces by life or relationships
2. "heal" — ἰάομαι (*iaomai*): to cure; usually refers to a progressive cure; often depicts a healing power that progressively reverses a condition over a period of time, or a sickness that is progressively healed rather than instantaneously healed
3. "deliverance" — ἄφεσις (*aphesis*): a release; a dismissal; to set free; to permanently loose
4. "captives" — αἰχμάλωτος (*aichmalotos*): captives; those taken captive at the point of a spear; those who are dragged into bondage; manipulated by bondage
5. "recovering of sight" — ἀνάβλεψις (*anablepsis*): the returning of one's sight; the restoration of sight; to see again
6. "blind" — τυφλός (*tuphlos*): blind; it doesn't just depict a person who is unable to see, but a person who has been intentionally blinded by someone else; can picture one whose eyes have been deliberately removed so that he is blinded; that individual hasn't just lost his sight, but he has no eyes with which to see
7. "set at liberty" — ἄφεσις (*aphesis*): a release; a dismissal; to permanently loose; to set free; in this case, from the detrimental effects of

a shattered life; the Greek speaks of a permanent release from the destructive effects of brokenness

8. "bruised" — τεθραυσμένους (*tethrausmenous*): to crush; to break down; depicts a person who has been shattered or fractured by life; pictures those whose lives have been continually split up and fragmented

9. "guide" — ὁδηγός (*hodegos*): a guide who shows a traveler the safest course through an unknown country; a guide who knows the safest, fastest, and most pleasurable route to take; a tour guide; a guide for the blind

10. "led" — ἄγω (*ago*): to lead: depicted animals led by a rope tied around their necks, that followed wherever their owner led them; the owner would "tug" and "pull" and the animal followed; to be led by a gentle tug or pull; this word forms the root for the Greek word ἀγών (*agon*), which describes an intense conflict, such as a struggle in a wrestling match or a struggle of the human will

SYNOPSIS

When David penned the powerful words of Psalm 23, he was not only comparing the Lord to a shepherd, but also calling himself a sheep. Imagine that! The mighty King David — the man who ruled Israel for 40 years and subdued all the enemies of God's people — likened himself to a helpless lamb that was totally dependent on the Lord to provide for his needs, protect him wherever he went, bring peace to his anxious heart, and restore his wounded soul.

The emphasis of this lesson:

The fifth divine promise from the Lord is supernatural guidance. The Spirit of God Himself lives inside of you and is ever ready to lead and direct you in the way you should go. If you will let Him, He will be your tour guide for a lifetime of adventure.

With a grateful heart of praise, David opened his mouth and rehearsed aloud the magnificence and faithfulness of our God. He proclaimed:

> The Lord is my shepherd; I shall not want. He maketh me to lie down in green pastures: he leadeth me beside the still waters. He restoreth my soul: he leadeth me in the paths of righteousness for his name's sake. Yea, though I walk through the valley

of the shadow of death, I will fear no evil: for thou art with me; thy rod and thy staff they comfort me. Thou preparest a table before me in the presence of mine enemies: thou anointest my head with oil; my cup runneth over. Surely goodness and mercy shall follow me all the days of my life: and I will dwell in the house of the Lord for ever.

— Psalm 23:1-6

What does God promise YOU, His beloved sheep, in this passage?

- **Supernatural provision (Psalm 23:1)**
- **Supernatural protection (Psalm 23:2)**
- **Supernatural peace (Psalm 23:2)**
- **Supernatural restoration (Psalm 23:3)**
- **Supernatural guidance (Psalm 23:3)**
- **Supernatural confidence (Psalm 23:4)**
- **Supernatural correction (Psalm 23:4)**
- **Supernatural prosperity (Psalm 23:5)**
- **Supernatural anointing/blessing (Psalm 23:5)**
- **Supernatural promise (Psalm 23:6)**

A Review of Jesus' Work as the Restorer of Our Souls

In Psalm 23:3, the Bible says that the Lord *restores our souls*. As we saw in Lesson 4, Jesus gave us a powerful description of His role as our Restorer in Luke 4:18 and 19, saying:

> The Spirit of the Lord is upon me, because he hath anointed me to preach the gospel to the poor; he hath sent me to heal the brokenhearted, to preach deliverance to the captives, and recovering of sight to the blind, to set at liberty them that are bruised, to preach the acceptable year of the Lord.

First, notice Jesus said He was anointed to **"preach the Gospel to the poor."** This lets us know that when the Word of God is declared, it packs the potential to be an economic game-changer in the lives of the poor.

Next, Jesus said He was sent to **"heal the brokenhearted."** We saw that the word "brokenhearted" is a translation of the Greek word *suntribo*, which is normally used to describe *the crushing of grapes with the feet* or *the smashing and grinding of bones into dust*. However, in this verse, it depicts people who have been walked on or crushed by others. They feel as though they have been trampled on or smashed to pieces by relationships or life itself. These are the "brokenhearted" Jesus came to *heal*.

The word "heal" here is the Greek word *iaomai*, which means *to cure* and usually refers to *a progressive cure*. It often depicts a healing power that progressively reverses a condition over a period of time, or a sickness that is progressively healed rather than instantaneously healed. When the Lord goes to work restoring our broken hearts, it is usually a process that takes time. But regardless of how long it takes, He vows to stay with us every step of the way until the restoration is completed.

Jesus went on to say that He came to **"preach deliverance to the captives"** (Luke 4:18). The word "deliverance" in Greek is the word *aphesis*, which describes *a permanent release* or *a dismissal*. The use of this word lets us know that Jesus is not into performing a temporary fix. The work He does is meant to be *permanent*. He came to permanently deliver, permanently set free, and provide permanent release to the "captives."

The term "captives" in Greek is a picture of *those taken captive at the point of a spear* or *those who are dragged into bondage or manipulated by bondage*. In this verse, the word "captives" can portray individuals bound by chemical addictions, sexual addictions, wrong thinking, or abusive relationships. Christ desires to permanently release these people from their imprisonment.

But that's not all. Jesus also included in His mission **"recovering of sight to the blind"** (Luke 4:18). The words "recovery of sight" is a translation of the Greek word *anablepsis*, which describes *the returning of one's sight* or *the restoration of sight*. So many people have been blind-sided by situations in life that they didn't see coming. Not only does Jesus reach down and pull these individuals out of the ditch, He also restores their sight so they can get back on the road to fulfilling their destiny.

This brings us to the word "blind," which is the Greek word *tuphlos*, and while it does describe one who is *blind*, it doesn't just depict a person who is unable to see. It actually denotes *someone who has been intentionally blinded by someone else*. This is a person whose eyes have been deliberately removed so that he is blinded. Thus, he hasn't just lost his sight; he no longer has eyes with which to see. These are the "blind" people to whom Jesus wants sight restored.

What other form of restoration does Jesus bring? The Bible says He is anointed by God to **"set at liberty them that are bruised"** (Luke 4:18). The words "set at liberty" are derived from the Greek word *aphesis* — the same word we saw translated as "deliverance" at the beginning of this verse. Again, it means *to permanently release, permanently dismiss, or permanently set free*. In this case, it means to permanently loose someone from the detrimental effects of a *bruised* or *shattered* life.

The meaning of the word "bruised," the Greek word *tethrausmenous*, means *to crush* or *to break down*. It depicts *one who has been shattered or fractured by life*; it is a picture of those whose lives have been continually split up and fragmented. This would include people who have been in and out of numerous relationships, those who have experienced divorce, and children of divorce or wards of the state that have been passed around from family to family. The Bible says Jesus came to permanently set free these precious people from the destructive effects of brokenness.

David knew firsthand what it felt like to be broken. He was the youngest of eight sons who suffered a great deal of rejection from his siblings, not to mention betrayal from two of his sons and marital problems with multiple wives. Although David had been wounded in his soul, he had personally tasted of the Lord's restoration power. That's why he declared, "The Lord is my shepherd… [and] He restoreth my soul…" (Psalm 23:1,3).

The Lord Promises Supernatural Guidance

The fifth promise the Lord makes to us as our Good Shepherd is found in the second part of Psalm 23:3, where David said, "…He leadeth me in the paths of righteousness for his name's sake." Just as a shepherd directs his flock where to go and where not to go, Jesus cares about us and desires to lead us through all of life.

God has given us numerous scriptures to tell us He is totally committed to giving us guidance and direction in our lives. Consider these powerful promises:

> I will instruct you and teach you in the way you should go; I will guide you with My eye.
> — Psalm 32:8 (*NKJV*)

> The Lord directs the steps of the godly. He delights in every detail of their lives.
> — Psalm 37:23 (*NLT*)

> You guide me with your counsel, leading me to a glorious destiny.
> — Psalm 73:24 (*NLT*)

> In all your ways acknowledge Him, and He shall direct your paths.
> — Proverbs 3:6 (*NKJV*)

Of all the ways in which God speaks to us and directs our steps, the Bible is foundational to them all. He has graciously given us His Word so we can know His mind, His will, and His ways. Scripture is full of His wisdom and His counsel. This is why David stated, "Your word is a lamp to my feet and a light to my path" (Psalm 119:105 *NKJV*). Through God's Word, our paths are confirmed and made clear.

The Holy Spirit Has Been Given as Our Divine Tour Guide

In addition to God's Word, He has also blessed us with the priceless gift of His Holy Spirit to lead us through life. Speaking of the Holy Spirit, Jesus said, "Howbeit when he, the Spirit of truth, is come, he will guide you into all truth…" (John 16:13). The word "guide" in this verse is the Greek word *hodegos*, and it is simply amazing! It is taken from the word *hodas*, the term for a *road*. When *hodas* becomes *hodegos*, it describes *one who knows all the roads*. Essentially, it is the Greek word for a *tour guide — one who shows a traveler the safest course through an unknown country*. This is a guide who knows the safest, fastest, and most pleasurable route to take.

What's interesting about this word *hodegos* — translated here as "guide" — is that it's the same word used to describe *a guide for the blind*. If someone was blind, they had to put all their trust in their guide to lead them safely and correctly to where they needed to go. By using this word, Jesus is saying, "Let the Holy Spirit be your eyes. Trust Him. He is the Spirit of truth and is able to see what you cannot see. He will never lead you astray."

It is no accident that Jesus chose the word *hodegos* (guide) to describe the work of the Holy Spirit. He is the greatest tour guide you will ever have. He knows what is in front of you because He has already been where He is leading you. He knows all the roads and the best routes to take and the ones you need to avoid. If you let Him lead, He will help you avoid countless demonic attacks and take you on the most exciting, most enjoyable journey ever!

If you are a born-again child of God, you have His guarantee to be led by His Spirit! Through the apostle Paul, God said, "For as many as are led by the Spirit of God, these are sons of God" (Romans 8:14 *NKJV*). The word "led" here is the Greek word *ago*, which means *to lead*. This word was used to depict animals led by a rope tied around their necks, and they followed wherever their owner led them. The owner would simply "tug" or "pull" on the rope, and the animal followed. What's interesting is that this word *ago* — translated here as "led" — forms the root for the Greek word *agon*, which describes *an intense conflict*, such as a struggle in a wrestling match or a struggle of the human will.

Probably one of the most important lessons we can learn from this word *ago* is revealed in a story Rick shared about a grandmother who lived on a very small piece of land on the outskirts of a little village in Latvia. Every morning, she would tie a rope around the neck of her cow and lead it off her property to the front of Rick's property, and that cow would obediently follow her. She would then pull a stake out of her pocket, tie the other end of the rope around it, and drive the stake into the ground. She then patted the cow on the back and said, "See you later," and went back home. Later that day as night began to fall, the grandmother returned, pulled the stake out of the ground, and took the rope and led the cow back home. Day after day, week after week, she did the same thing. One day, opportunity arose, and Rick asked one of his neighboring friends, "Why does that huge cow so amiably follow that little old lady?" The neighbor answered, "Because that cow has been trained to follow that grandmother since it was a wee calf."

Friend, the best time to learn how to follow the leading of the Holy Spirit is early in life. It is one of the very best things you can train your children to do. The good news is, even if you are further along in age, you can still learn how to listen and submit to the leading of the Holy Spirit. The more you obediently follow His gentle tug or pull, the less of a struggle it will be. He will show you what to say and what not to say — what to do and what not to do. He will protect you from danger and help you make the best decisions in whatever circumstance you face. The Lord is your shepherd who leads you in the paths of righteousness for His name's sake! When you obediently follow Him and experience success, it brings glory to the name of Jesus.

In our next lesson, we will explore the sixth promise the Lord has made to us — the guarantee of supernatural confidence found in Psalm 23:4.

STUDY QUESTIONS

> Study to shew thyself approved unto God, a workman that needeth not to be ashamed, rightly dividing the word of truth.
> — 2 Timothy 2:15

1. The Bible says, "If any of you needs wisdom to know what you should do, you should ask God, and he will give it to you. God is generous to everyone and doesn't find fault with them" (James 1:5 *GW*). What do these promises from Scripture say to you about God's desire and ability to lead and direct your steps?

    - Psalm 25:9,12 and 48:14
    - Isaiah 30:21
    - Jeremiah 33:3
    - Proverbs 3:5-8

2. In what areas of your everyday life — major or minor — do you need the Holy Spirit to show you what to do? Do you trust Him to give you the direction you need? If you're struggling to trust Him, read God's promise to you in Psalm 84:11 and Jesus' words in Matthew 7:7-11.

3. Being led by the Lord is not a one-time event, but a lifelong adventure with seasons that are beautiful, and others that are extremely hard — even when He's leading us through them. If you're currently in one of the most difficult times of your life, take a few moments to soak in the hope of Isaiah 43:1 and 2, and Second Timothy 4:18.

PRACTICAL APPLICATION

> But be ye doers of the word, and not hearers only,
> deceiving your own selves.
> —James 1:22

1. When was the last time you felt like God gave you specific guidance on something? What was it about? Did you trust Him? If not, what kept you from taking the step He was directing you to take?
2. In what areas of your life do you find it difficult to let the Lord lead you? Where do you struggle most to relinquish control? Pray and ask God to show you why this area is such a struggle, and to give you the grace you need to trust Him with it.
3. One of the greatest roles of the Holy Spirit in your life is serving as your divine tour guide. He is the one who knows all the roads — the ones to take and the ones to avoid. Where do you feel totally blind and need the Holy Spirit to be your eyes? (Check out Isaiah 42:16.)

LESSON 6

TOPIC

God's Supernatural Confidence

SCRIPTURES

1. **Psalm 23:1-6** — The Lord is my shepherd; I shall not want. He maketh me to lie down in green pastures: he leadeth me beside the still waters. He restoreth my soul: he leadeth me in the paths of righteousness for his name's sake. Yea, though I walk through the valley of the shadow of death, I will fear no evil: for thou art with me; thy rod and thy staff they comfort me. Thou preparest a table before me in the presence of mine enemies: thou anointest my head with oil; my cup runneth over. Surely goodness and mercy shall follow me all the days of my life: and I will dwell in the house of the Lord for ever.
2. **Psalm 5:12** — For thou, Lord, wilt bless the righteous; with favour wilt thou compass him as with a shield.

3. **Psalm 17:8,9** — Keep me as the apple of the eye, hide me under the shadow of thy wings, From the wicked that oppress me, from my deadly enemies, who compass me about.
4. **Psalm 17:13** — Arise, O Lord, disappoint him, cast him down: deliver my soul from the wicked....
5. **Psalm 18:1-3** — To the chief Musician, A Psalm of David, the servant of the Lord, who spake unto the Lord the words of this song in the day that the Lord delivered him from the hand of all his enemies, and from the hand of Saul. And he said, I will love thee, O Lord, my strength. The Lord is my rock, and my fortress, and my deliverer; my God, my strength, in whom I will trust; my buckler, and the horn of my salvation, and my high tower. I will call upon the Lord, who is worthy to be praised: so shall I be saved from mine enemies.
6. **Psalm 18:6** — In my distress I called upon the Lord, and cried unto my God: he heard my voice out of his temple, and my cry came before him, even into his ears.
7. **Psalm 18:19** — He brought me forth also into a large place; he delivered me, because he delighted in me.
8. **Psalm 18:36** — Thou hast enlarged my steps under me, that my feet did not slip.
9. **Psalm 21:11** — For they intended evil against thee: they imagined a mischievous device, which they are not able to perform.
10. **Psalm 22:19** — But be not thou far from me, O Lord: O my strength, haste thee to help me.
11. **Psalm 27:1** — The Lord is my light and my salvation; whom shall I fear? the Lord is the strength of my life; of whom shall I be afraid?
12. **Psalm 31:1-4** — In thee, O Lord, do I put my trust; let me never be ashamed: deliver me in thy righteousness. Bow down thine ear to me; deliver me speedily: be thou my strong rock, for an house of defence to save me. For thou art my rock and my fortress; therefore for thy name's sake lead me, and guide me. Pull me out of the net that they have laid privily for me: for thou art my strength.
13. **Psalm 31:20** — Thou shalt hide them in the secret of thy presence from the pride of man: thou shalt keep them secretly in a pavilion from the strife of tongues.
14. **Psalm 32:7** — Thou art my hiding place; thou shalt preserve me from trouble; thou shalt compass me about with songs of deliverance. Selah.

15. **Psalm 37:23,24** — The steps of a good man are ordered by the Lord: and he delighteth in his way. Though he fall, he shall not be utterly cast down: for the Lord upholdeth him with his hand.
16. **Psalm 56:2-4** — Mine enemies would daily swallow me up: for they be many that fight against me, O thou most High. What time I am afraid, I will trust in thee. In God I will praise his word, in God I have put my trust; I will not fear what flesh can do unto me.
17. **Psalm 57:1-7** — Be merciful unto me, O God, be merciful unto me: For my soul trusteth in thee: yea, in the shadow of thy wings will I make my refuge, until these calamities be overpast. I will cry unto God most high; unto God that performeth all things for me. He shall send from heaven, and save me from the reproach of him that would swallow me up. Selah. God shall send forth his mercy and his truth. My soul is among lions: And I lie even among them that are set on fire, even the sons of men, whose teeth are spears and arrows, and their tongue a sharp sword. Be thou exalted, O God, above the heavens; let thy glory be above all the earth. They have prepared a net for my steps; my soul is bowed down: they have digged a pit before me, into the midst whereof they are fallen themselves. Selah. My heart is fixed, O God, my heart is fixed: I will sing and give praise.
18. **Psalm 61:1-4** — Hear my cry, O God; attend unto my prayer. From the end of the earth will I cry unto thee, when my heart is overwhelmed: lead me to the rock that is higher than I. For thou hast been a shelter for me, and a strong tower from the enemy. I will abide in thy tabernacle for ever: I will trust in the covert of thy wings. Selah.
19. **Psalm 71:1-3** — In thee, O Lord, do I put my trust: let me never be put to confusion. Deliver me in thy righteousness, and cause me to escape: incline thine ear unto me, and save me. Be thou my strong habitation, whereunto I may continually resort: Thou hast given commandment to save me; for thou art my rock and my fortress.
20. **Psalm 112:7** — He shall not be afraid of evil tidings: his heart is fixed, trusting in the Lord.
21. **Psalm 34:19** — Many are the afflictions of the righteous, but the Lord delivers him out of them all.
22. **Proverbs 3:5,6** (*NKJV*) — Trust in the Lord with all your heart, And lean not on your own understanding; In all your ways acknowledge Him, And He shall direct your paths.

23. **Psalm 4:8** — I will both lay me down in peace, and sleep: For thou, Lord, only makest me dwell in safety.

GREEK WORDS

There are no Greek words in this lesson.

SYNOPSIS

One of the greatest promises God has made to us as believers is to be with us at all times. When Jacob came to Bethel, God appeared to him in a dream and said, "Behold, I am with you and will keep you wherever you go…" (Genesis 28:15 *NKJV*). After Moses died, God told Joshua, "…As I was with Moses, so I will be with you. I will not leave you nor forsake you" (Joshua 1:5 *NKJV*). Likewise, just before Jesus ascended to Heaven, He told His disciples, "…And, lo, I am with you always, even unto the end of the world. Amen" (Matthew 28:20).

What God promised Jacob, Joshua, and the disciples, He also promises to *you*. Remember, He has no favorites and does not show partiality (*see* Acts 10:34). Knowing that God is always with us and will never leave us is the greatest source of confidence we will ever have!

The emphasis of this lesson:

Again and again, God — our Shepherd — promises to be with us and never leave us. Having a heart revelation of His continual abiding presence releases the gift of supernatural confidence in us.

It has been said that Psalm 23 was written by David after he transitioned into his role as the anointed king of Israel. After many years of ruthlessly being hunted down by King Saul, he was able to look back on God's faithfulness to protect him and provide for him through some of the darkest hours of his life. Thus, Psalm 23 is David's declaration of the Lord's unrivalled dependability. He said:

> **The Lord is my shepherd; I shall not want. He maketh me to lie down in green pastures: he leadeth me beside the still waters. He restoreth my soul: he leadeth me in the paths of righteousness for his name's sake. Yea, though I walk through the valley of the shadow of death, I will fear no evil: for thou art with me; thy rod and thy staff they comfort me. Thou preparest a table**

before me in the presence of mine enemies: thou anointest my head with oil; my cup runneth over. Surely goodness and mercy shall follow me all the days of my life: and I will dwell in the house of the Lord for ever.

— Psalm 23:1-6

Thus far, we have closely examined the first five promises in this passage, which are:

- Supernatural provision (Psalm 23:1)
- Supernatural protection (Psalm 23:2)
- Supernatural peace (Psalm 23:2)
- Supernatural restoration (Psalm 23:3)
- Supernatural guidance (Psalm 23:3)

In the remaining lessons, we will focus on five additional promises, including:

- Supernatural confidence (Psalm 23:4)
- Supernatural correction (Psalm 23:4)
- Supernatural prosperity (Psalm 23:5)
- Supernatural anointing/blessing (Psalm 23:5)
- Supernatural promise (Psalm 23:6)

Where Are You Placing Your Confidence?

In Webster's original 1828 dictionary, the primary definition for the word "confidence" is *a trusting, or reliance; an assurance of mind or firm belief in the integrity, stability or veracity of another, or in the truth and reality of a fact.*[1] Since the beginning of time, people have placed their confidence in all sorts of things, including money, material possessions, education, personal connections, the government, and even themselves. Although all of these are helpful and needed in some way to make it through life, they are fleeting and unreliable.

Only one thing is unchanging and reliable at all times, through all circumstances, through all generations, and that is *God*. David understood this, which is why he was able to boldly proclaim, "Yea, though I walk through the valley of the shadow of death, I will fear no evil: for thou art with me…" (Psalm 23:4). It's important to notice that David didn't say, "Even though I *camp out* [or *live*] in the valley of the shadow of death…." He said that he *walked through* the valley.

The fact is, when you read the book of Psalms and the history of David's life in First and Second Samuel, it becomes quite clear that he endured many hardships throughout his life. Yet through all his dark moments, he continued to place his hope and trust in the Lord, his Shepherd. God desires that we do the same.

Whether you are experiencing challenges in your marriage, your family, your finances, on your job, or with your health, God is with you every step of the way! Like David, you are not staying in that troublesome place. You are walking through it. And as we noted in the introduction, knowing God is always with you and will never leave you provides a rock-solid confidence that you can make it through anything!

The Psalms of David: An Intimate Picture of Dependence on God

Romans 15:4 (*NKJV*) says, "For whatever things were written before were written for our learning, that we through the patience and comfort of the Scriptures might have hope." God has given us His Word as a source of wisdom and instruction. Hence, David's words in the Psalms — many of which he wrote during the dark seasons of his life — are a priceless resource from which we can learn and receive comfort and hope as we walk through our own times of trouble.

The following key passages have been a tremendous source of strength and encouragement for Rick and Denise as well as countless other believers through the centuries. We believe they will be a wealth of strength and hope to you too.

God Is Our Shield Against the Wicked

Psalm 5:12 says, "For thou, Lord, wilt bless the righteous; with favour wilt thou compass him as with a shield." Here God promises to be a *shield* of favor that surrounds you and protects you against evil attacks.

In **Psalm 17:8 and 9**, David prayed to the Lord saying, "Keep me as the apple of the eye, hide me under the shadow of thy wings, from the wicked that oppress me, from my deadly enemies, who compass me about."

Whenever you feel like you're surrounded by wicked enemies, you can pray a prayer just like this one that David prayed when Saul was chasing him and trying to kill him.

In **Psalm 17:13**, David continued his prayer by saying, "Arise, O Lord, disappoint him, cast him down: deliver my soul from the wicked...."

God Is Our Rock

When you turn to **Psalm 18**, there is a note just before the text begins that reads, "To the chief Musician, A Psalm of David, the servant of the Lord, who spake unto the Lord the words of this song in the day that the Lord delivered him from the hand of all his enemies, and from the hand of Saul."

What did David say? He said, "I will love thee, O Lord, my strength. The Lord is my rock, and my fortress, and my deliverer; my God, my strength, in whom I will trust; my buckler, and the horn of my salvation, and my high tower" (**Psalm 18:1,2**).

Over and over throughout the psalms, David often prayed, "Lord, set me upon a rock." The reason for this request was that by being set upon a rock, he was placed high above and out of the reach of his enemies. Another phrase David often proclaimed was, "Lord, You are my rock and my fortress." This was David's declaration of trust in God and it can be ours as well — that God is the ultimate stronghold of safety in times of trouble.

You Can Call on the Lord Anytime

Whenever David was in distress, he knew what to do. In **Psalm 18:3**, he said, "I will call upon the Lord, who is worthy to be praised: so shall I be saved from mine enemies." Then in **Psalm 18:6** he announced, "In my distress I called upon the Lord, and cried unto my God: he heard my voice out of his temple, and my cry came before him, even into his ears."

How did God respond to David's cry? In **Psalm 18:19**, David tells us, "He brought me forth also into a large place; he delivered me, because he delighted in me." Clearly, when David was being hunted down by King Saul, he felt entrapped. But God heard his cry and came down from Heaven to deliver David.

In **Psalm 18:36**, David went on to say, "Thou hast enlarged my steps under me, that my feet did not slip." When you feel like your feet are slipping off the path and you can't seem to get any traction, you can pray to the Lord as David did, and He will enable you to regain your footing!

God Will Frustrate the Plans of the Wicked

David was no stranger to the schemes of Satan working through evil men. Yet he remained confident in the Lord. In **Psalm 21:11**, he said, "For they intended evil against thee: they imagined a mischievous device, which they are not able to perform." The plans of the wicked never succeeded against David because of the Lord's divine intervention.

Whenever David was being attacked, he turned to the Lord in prayer. For example, in **Psalm 22:19**, he prayed, "But be not thou far from me, O Lord: O my strength, haste thee to help me." And because of God's track record of arriving just in the nick of time and thwarting his enemies' plans, David repeatedly made declarations like this one in **Psalm 27:1**: "The Lord is my light and my salvation; whom shall I fear? the Lord is the strength of my life; of whom shall I be afraid?" The confidence he had in the Lord is certainly evident in verses like these.

The Lord Is Our Mighty Deliverer

In **Psalm 31:1-4**, David lifted his voice to God and said, "In thee, O Lord, do I put my trust; let me never be ashamed: deliver me in thy righteousness. Bow down thine ear to me; deliver me speedily: be thou my strong rock, for an house of defence to save me. For thou art my rock and my fortress; therefore for thy name's sake lead me, and guide me. Pull me out of the net that they have laid privily for me: for thou art my strength."

Here again, we see David referring to the Lord as his "rock" and "fortress." In David's mind, only the Lord could successfully deliver him from all the traps the enemy had set. History reveals that he was never disappointed. God always came through for him, and He will always come through for you.

The Lord Is Our Hiding Place

Sometimes when David saw trouble coming, he would ask the Lord to hide him out of the sight of his enemies. We see this in **Psalm 31:20**, where he said, "Thou shalt hide them in the secret of thy presence from the pride of man: thou shalt keep them secretly in a pavilion from the strife of tongues."

You may wonder, *What is the strife of tongues?* This is a reference to the times when people speak evil, nasty things about you, which are often blatant lies. This verse lets us know that we can pray and ask the Lord to protect us from the verbal assaults people bring against us. As David declared in **Psalm 32:7**, we too can proclaim: "Thou art my hiding place; thou shalt preserve me from trouble; thou shalt compass me about with songs of deliverance. Selah."

Your Steps Are Directed by God

Have you ever wondered what God's will is for your life? You can find comfort and reassurance in **Psalm 37:23**, which says, "The steps of a good man are ordered by the Lord: and he delighteth in his way." This verse reveals that even when you go through difficult times, God is still at work directing your steps and straightening out the path before you.

David then adds in **Psalm 37:24**, "Though he fall, he shall not be utterly cast down: for the Lord upholdeth him with his hand." What an encouragement! Even when we mess up, God is holding us up with His mighty hand of strength. This truth is reaffirmed in Isaiah 41:10.

The Lord Is Worthy of Your Trust

At one point when David was running for his life, he was captured by the Philistines. After the experience, he wrote **Psalm 56:2-4** in which he said, "Mine enemies would daily swallow me up: For they be many that fight against me, O thou most High. What time I am afraid, I will trust in thee. In God I will praise his word, in God I have put my trust; I will not fear what flesh can do unto me."

In this passage, we see another phrase David speaks throughout the Psalms: "I will not fear what flesh can do unto me." There is no way David could repeatedly make such a bold statement unless he had a supernatural confidence that the Lord was truly *for* him. Through all of life's experiences, he had learned no one could stand against him because God was standing with him.

God Is a God of Great Mercy

First Samuel 23 and 24 tell of the time David was hiding out in a cave in desert of En Gedi. It was during this period that he came extremely close to be found and captured by King Saul. **Psalm 57:1-7** captures the intensity of these moments in which David appealed to God and said:

Be merciful unto me, O God, be merciful unto me: For my soul trusteth in thee: yea, in the shadow of thy wings will I make my refuge, until these calamities be overpast. I will cry unto God most high; unto God that performeth all things for me. He shall send from heaven, and save me from the reproach of him that would swallow me up. Selah. God shall send forth his mercy and his truth.

My soul is among lions: And I lie even among them that are set on fire, even the sons of men, whose teeth are spears and arrows, and their tongue a sharp sword. Be thou exalted, O God, above the heavens; let thy glory be above all the earth. They have prepared a net for my steps; my soul is bowed down: they have digged a pit before me, into the midst whereof they are fallen themselves. Selah. My heart is fixed, O God, my heart is fixed: I will sing and give praise.

Notice David said he was "among lions…even the sons of men, whose teeth are spears and arrows, and their tongue a sharp sword" (Psalm 57:4). Here again he is speaking about people who were verbally assaulting him and ripping him to shreds with their words. If there are people talking about you — or digging a trap for you to fall in — you can be confident that they themselves will be ensnared by their words and fall into the very pit they have dug for you! Through all of this, David remained stable. Why? The answer is in Psalm 57:7: He had *fixed his heart* on God — determined to hold tightly to God's promises.

The Lord Will Hear and Answer Your Cry

David gives us a powerful prayer for help in **Psalm 61:1-4**. With a sense of desperation, he lifts his voice and says, "Hear my cry, O God; attend unto my prayer. From the end of the earth will I cry unto thee, when my heart is overwhelmed: lead me to the rock that is higher than I. For thou hast been a shelter for me, and a strong tower from the enemy. I will abide in thy tabernacle for ever: I will trust in the covert of thy wings. Selah." Again, David pleads with God to place him on the rock, out of reach of the enemy.

He offers a similar prayer in **Psalm 71:1-3**. Here David calls out, "In thee, O Lord, do I put my trust: let me never be put to confusion. Deliver me in thy righteousness, and cause me to escape: incline thine ear unto me, and save me. Be thou my strong habitation, whereunto I may continually resort: Thou hast given commandment to save me; for thou art my rock and my fortress."

Fixing Your Heart on God Is the Key to Victory

As we saw in Psalm 57:7, David had discovered the key to victory through all the life-threatening challenges he faced: He learned to fix his heart on God. We see this principle repeated in **Psalm 112:7**, which says, "He shall not be afraid of evil tidings: his heart is fixed, trusting in the Lord."

The fact is, in this life we are going to experience trouble and even tribulation. Jesus Himself told us this in John 16:33. But with His next breath, He proclaimed, "…But be of good cheer, I have overcome the world." David understood this truth, which is what prompted him to write **Psalm 34:19**, which says, "Many are the afflictions of the righteous, but the Lord delivers him out of them all."

Did David experience times of fear? Most definitely. But he learned to focus on the Lord, his Shepherd, not on the problems. David's words show us the care of our Good Shepherd whose influence transcends even the worst that life can throw at us. Although being a follower of Jesus does not make us exempt from the challenges of life, our Good Shepherd is an ever-present help in time of need — and He carries a rod for dealing with our enemies.

Friend, get your focus off your enemies and the problems all around you and fix your heart and mind on Jesus, your Good Shepherd. Learn to put your trust in God and His Word moment by moment, day by day. He has not failed you in the past, and He will not fail you in the future. "Trust in the Lord with all your heart, And lean not on your own understanding; In all your ways acknowledge Him, And He shall direct your paths" (Proverbs 3:5,6 *NKJV*). When you know that the Lord is your Shepherd who is constantly watching over you, you can learn to say as David said, "I will both lay me down in peace, and sleep: For thou, Lord, only makest me dwell in safety" (Psalm 4:8).

STUDY QUESTIONS

> Study to shew thyself approved unto God, a workman that needeth
> not to be ashamed, rightly dividing the word of truth.
> —2 Timothy 2:15

1. Of all the passages in Psalms presented in this lesson, which one (ones) encouraged you the most? What other verses — not included in this teaching — have been a source of strength and hope to you? How do they instill confidence in you that God is always at your side?
2. David had a supernatural confidence that the Lord was truly *for* him. Do you know — *really know* — that God is *for you*? Take time to meditate on this New Testament promise and ask the Holy Spirit to infuse into your soul this game-changing revelation.
3. "What then shall we say to [all] this? If God is for us, who [can be] against us? [Who can be our foe, if God is on our side?] He who did not withhold or spare [even] His own Son but gave Him up for us all, will He not also with Him freely and graciously give us all [other] things?" (Romans 8:31,32 *AMPC*)
4. Through all the life-threatening challenges David faced, He learned to *fix his heart* on God (*see* Psalm 57:7). Also read Psalm 141:8; Hebrews 12:1-4; and Second Corinthians 4:17,18. How do these verses help you better understand the importance of fixing your focus on Jesus?

PRACTICAL APPLICATION

> But be ye doers of the word, and not hearers only,
> deceiving your own selves.
> —James 1:22

1. The word "confidence" is defined as *a trusting, or reliance; an assurance of mind or firm belief in the integrity, stability, or veracity of another*. Be honest: In what have you been putting your confidence? Is it the government or the amount of money you have stored up in the bank? Is it your job or the people you know? Is it your education, your talents, or your life's experiences? Are you seeing why it is foolish and even dangerous for you to put confidence in these things?
2. In Psalm 23:4, David declared, "Yea, though I walk through the valley of the shadow of death, I will fear no evil: for thou art with me...." Are you presently walking through a dark valley? If so, what are you

facing? What thoughts of fear is the enemy bringing against you? How is this teaching helping to dismantle those fears and see God's greatness more clearly?

---

[1] *An American Dictionary of the English Language*, by Noah Webster, LL.D. (The Foundation for American Christian Education: San Francisco, CA: 2000).

LESSON 7

TOPIC
God's Supernatural Protection and Correction

SCRIPTURES
1. **Psalm 23:1-6** — The Lord is my shepherd; I shall not want. He maketh me to lie down in green pastures: he leadeth me beside the still waters. He restoreth my soul: he leadeth me in the paths of righteousness for his name's sake. Yea, though I walk through the valley of the shadow of death, I will fear no evil: for thou art with me; thy rod and thy staff they comfort me. Thou preparest a table before me in the presence of mine enemies: thou anointest my head with oil; my cup runneth over. Surely goodness and mercy shall follow me all the days of my life: and I will dwell in the house of the Lord for ever.
2. **John 10:11-13** — I am the good shepherd: the good shepherd giveth his life for the sheep. But he that is an hireling, and not the shepherd, whose own the sheep are not, seeth the wolf coming, and leaveth the sheep, and fleeth: and the wolf catcheth them, and scattereth the sheep. The hireling fleeth, because he is an hireling, and careth not for the sheep
3. **1 Samuel 17:34-36** — And David said unto Saul, Thy servant kept his father's sheep, and there came a lion, and a bear, and took a lamb out of the flock: And I went out after him, and smote him, and delivered it out of his mouth: and when he arose against me, I caught him by

his beard, and smote him, and slew him. Thy servant slew both the lion and the bear....

4. **1 Samuel 17:34-36** (*NLT*) — But David persisted. "I have been taking care of my father's sheep and goats," he said. "When a lion or a bear comes to steal a lamb from the flock, I go after it with a club and rescue the lamb from its mouth. If the animal turns on me, I catch it by the jaw and club it to death. I have done this to both lions and bears...."

5. **Isaiah 59:1** — Behold, the Lord's hand is not shortened, that it cannot save....

6. **Psalm 51:1-4** — Have mercy upon me, O God, according to thy lovingkindness: according unto the multitude of thy tender mercies blot out my transgressions. Wash me throughly from mine iniquity, and cleanse me from my sin. For I acknowledge my transgressions: and my sin is ever before me. Against thee, thee only, have I sinned, and done this evil in thy sight: that thou mightest be justified when thou speakest, and be clear when thou judgest.

7. **Psalm 51:7-12** — Purge me with hyssop, and I shall be clean: wash me, and I shall be whiter than snow. Make me to hear joy and gladness; that the bones which thou hast broken may rejoice. Hide thy face from my sins, and blot out all mine iniquities. Create in me a clean heart, O God; and renew a right spirit within me. Cast me not away from thy presence; and take not thy holy spirit from me. Restore unto me the joy of thy salvation; and uphold me with thy free spirit.

GREEK WORDS

1. "hireling" — **μισθωτός** (*misthotos*): one who only works to get a salary
2. "shepherd" — **ποιμήν** (*poimen*): a shepherd; the feeder, protector, and ruler of a flock of people
3. "wolf" — **λύκος** (*lukos*): a wolf: applied figuratively to cruel, greedy, rapacious, destructive men; the word used to describe prostitutes who sold themselves; hence, not God-called leaders, but those who will sell themselves for gain and only stick around as long as there is something to be gained
4. "fleeth" — **φεύγω** (*pheugo*): to flee, to take flight, to run away, to run as fast as possible, or to escape; picture one's feet flying as he runs from a situation

5. "catcheth" — ἁρπάζω (*harpadzo*): to seize; to snatch; to steal or rob
6. "scatters" — σκορπίζω (*skorpidzo*): to scatter; related to σκορπίος (*skorpios*), the word for a scorpion; indicates the sheep scatter when they feel stung by a person or situation
7. "careth" — μέλει (*melei*): a care; depicts a deep concern; used positively to pay serious attention to something

SYNOPSIS

In our last lesson, we focused on David's words in Psalm 23:4, where he boldly declared, "Yea, though I walk through the valley of the shadow of death, I will fear no evil: for thou art with me…." In addition to the supernatural confidence that came from knowing God was always with him, David also had confidence in the Lord's protection because of what He carried in His hand. Psalm 23:4 concludes with David saying, "…Thy rod and thy staff they comfort me." Every good shepherd has a rod and staff, including the Lord. It is with the rod and staff that the shepherd protects and corrects his sheep.

The emphasis of this lesson:

The rod and staff in the hand of our Shepherd is for our protection and correction. When we get out of line, He uses His staff to prod us back into the right place. And when enemy forces come against us, the rod is used to beat them away.

Many people know that David's first job was to tend his father's sheep. But did you know that he held at least three other occupations in his life? It's true. In addition to reigning as the King of Israel for 40 years, David also served as a military commander under King Saul, and before that he was Saul's court musician. It was from his years as a shepherd and his experience as a skilled musician that he wrote the Twenty-Third Psalm, which says:

> The Lord is my shepherd; I shall not want. He maketh me to lie down in green pastures: he leadeth me beside the still waters. He restoreth my soul: he leadeth me in the paths of righteousness for his name's sake. Yea, though I walk through the valley of the shadow of death, I will fear no evil: for thou art with me; thy rod and thy staff they comfort me. Thou preparest a table before me in the presence of mine enemies: thou anointest my

head with oil; my cup runneth over. Surely goodness and mercy shall follow me all the days of my life: and I will dwell in the house of the Lord for ever.

— Psalm 23:1-6

Before you read on, pause and see if you can name the six promises in Psalm 23 we have already studied. Here they are again for your review:

- **Supernatural provision (Psalm 23:1)**
- **Supernatural protection (Psalm 23:2)**
- **Supernatural peace (Psalm 23:2)**
- **Supernatural restoration (Psalm 23:3)**
- **Supernatural guidance (Psalm 23:3)**
- **Supernatural confidence (Psalm 23:4)**

In the upcoming lessons, we will explore four more promises, including:

- **Supernatural correction (Psalm 23:4)**
- **Supernatural prosperity (Psalm 23:5)**
- **Supernatural anointing/blessing (Psalm 23:5)**
- **Supernatural promise (Psalm 23:6)**

The Difference Between the Good Shepherd and a 'Hireling'

The rod and staff are vital tools for any shepherd as they aid him in protecting and correcting his sheep. Very often this is one combined instrument with two different ends. One end of this long staff is often shaped like a hook, and it is used for grabbing sheep and pulling them back into place when they are out of line. The other end is basically straight and used to beat off — or kill — any predators that are trying to attack the sheep.

When David said that God's rod and staff comforted him, he was letting us know that our Shepherd has what He needs to not only direct and correct us when we're out of line, but also to effectively beat off any enemy that attempts to attack us. Jesus speaks of the tenacity of the shepherd when a wolf comes to attack the flock in John's gospel. He begins by announcing:

> I am the good shepherd: the good shepherd giveth his life for the sheep.
>
> —John 10:11

As we noted in a previous lesson, the original Greek text of this verse says, "I am the shepherd, the good one...." This is the equivalent of Jesus saying, "I am the best shepherd that exists...." Then He says of Himself, "...The good shepherd giveth his life for the sheep." In other words, He is going to do whatever is necessary to feed, nurture, and defend His flock. Jesus then goes on to tell us the difference between a good shepherd and a bad shepherd, which he calls a "hireling":

> But he that is an hireling, and not the shepherd, whose own the sheep are not, seeth the wolf coming, and leaveth the sheep, and fleeth: and the wolf catcheth them, and scattereth the sheep. The hireling fleeth, because he is an hireling, and careth not for the sheep.
>
> —John 10:12,13

There are six very important words to understand in this passage.

First, notice the word **"hireling."** It appears three times in two verses and is a translation of the Greek word *misthotos*, which means *one who only works to get a salary*. This person is not *called* to be a shepherd; they are merely filling a position to collect a paycheck.

Second, we see the word **"shepherd,"** which is the Greek word *poimen*, the word for *a shepherd*. It describes *the feeder, protector, and ruler of a flock of people*. This person is so committed to those under his care that he is willing to invest his entire life and even lay his life down for their betterment and safety.

Next, we see the word **"wolf"** — the Greek term *lukos*, which describes a wolf. When applied figuratively, it depicts *cruel, greedy, rapacious, destructive men*. What's fascinating about the word *lukos* is that it was used by Romans and Greeks to describe a particular group of prostitutes who sold themselves and howled during the night to attract the attention of men and lure them into their lairs.

The use of this word *lukos* — translated here as "wolf" — lets us know these are not God-called leaders, but those who will sell themselves for gain and only stick around as long as there is something to be gained.

These are men in ministry who have ulterior motives and are willing to prostitute or sell themselves to get something out of the people.

Jesus said that when a hireling sees a wolf show up, he **"fleeth."** This word "fleeth" in Greek is the term *pheugo*, which means *to flee*, *to take flight*, *to run away*, *to run as fast as possible*, or *to escape*. It pictures one's feet flying as he runs from a situation. When a wolf shows up and comes against the sheep, the hireling takes off running.

With the sheep left unprotected, the Bible says the wolf **"catcheth"** the sheep. This word "catcheth" is a translation of the Greek word *harpadzo*, which means *to seize*; *to snatch*; *to steal* or *rob*. Not only does the wolf catch the sheep, but he also **"scatters"** them. "Scatters" is the Greek word *skorpidzo*, which means *to scatter*, and is closely related to the Greek word *skorpios*, the word for a *scorpion*. The use of this word indicates that sheep scatter when they feel stung by a person or situation.

Lastly, Jesus said, "The hireling fleeth, because he is an hireling, and careth not for the sheep" (John 10:13). The word **"careth"** here is the Greek word *melei*, and it depicts *a deep concern*. When used positively, the word *melei* means to pay serious attention to something. But the hireling doesn't care for the sheep. All he cares about is himself and getting his paycheck.

In contrast, Jesus — the Good Shepherd — cares about us! When the wolf comes, Jesus doesn't run away. He stays right by us and defends us with His very life. He has a rod and a staff to take care of us and to rescue us from the mouths of predators.

David Understood the Purpose of the Rod and Staff

David was very familiar with the power of the rod and staff because he had been a shepherd to his father's sheep. Just before his face-off with Goliath, the giant from Gath, David spoke to King Saul and described his experiences as a shepherd. When the king was hesitant to letting David fight the giant, the Bible says:

> **But David persisted. 'I have been taking care of my father's sheep and goats,' he said. 'When a lion or a bear comes to steal a lamb from the flock, I go after it with a club and rescue the lamb**

from its mouth. If the animal turns on me, I catch it by the jaw and club it to death. I have done this to both lions and bears....'
— 1 Samuel 17:34-36 (*NLT*)

David knew that the sheep were safe when he had his rod in his hand. When any predators came against his sheep, he would use his rod like a club and beat the intruders — to death if necessary. Likewise, David was also comforted when he thought about the rod that his Shepherd carried. He knew that the Lord would use His rod to beat down any enemy that came against him.

David also knew the second purpose for the rod and staff, and that was to bring correction to the sheep. Remember, one end of the staff was shaped like a hook, and it was used to reach down and rescue a sheep that had fallen or to help it get out of a ditch and back on its feet again. If a sheep needed a gentle tap — to keep from putting itself in danger or to keep it from heading in a wrong direction — the rod became an extension of the shepherd's caring hands.

Make no mistake: God's loving hands are intimately involved in caring for us. The prophet Isaiah said, "Behold, the Lord's hand is not shortened, that it cannot save..." (Isaiah 59:1). When we're heading in the wrong direction, the Lord will use His rod and staff to prod us back onto the right path, and if necessary, to correct us more sternly. Always remember, God's correction provides protection.

David Was Personally Acquainted With the Lord's Correction

When David had committed adultery with Bathsheba and then had her husband, Uriah, murdered, the Lord sent Nathan the prophet to call David to account for his actions. David wrote about God's correction in his life in Psalm 51. In verses 1 through 4, He cried out:

> **Have mercy upon me, O God, according to thy lovingkindness: according unto the multitude of thy tender mercies blot out my transgressions.**
>
> **Wash me throughly from mine iniquity, and cleanse me from my sin.**
>
> **For I acknowledge my transgressions: and my sin is ever before me.**

> Against thee, thee only, have I sinned, and done this evil in thy sight: that thou mightest be justified when thou speakest, and be clear when thou judgest.

Indeed, David was a broken man when God brought correction to him. Yet, he owned up to his dreadful actions and did not run from the Lord's chastisement. In Psalm 51:7-12, he went on to say:

> Purge me with hyssop, and I shall be clean: wash me, and I shall be whiter than snow.
>
> Make me to hear joy and gladness; that the bones which thou hast broken may rejoice.
>
> Hide thy face from my sins, and blot out all mine iniquities.
>
> Create in me a clean heart, O God; and renew a right spirit within me.
>
> Cast me not away from thy presence; and take not thy holy spirit from me.
>
> Restore unto me the joy of thy salvation; and uphold me with thy free spirit.

Although God's correction in David's life was so strong it made him feel as if his bones had been broken (verse 8), he knew that God loved him and he needed to be disciplined in order for him to be placed back on track with God's will for his life.

Friend, let the Lord use His rod and staff in your life. It will provide protection against the enemy's attacks, and also bring correction when and where you need it most. In our next lesson, we will learn about God's supernatural prosperity and how He prepares a table of provision in the presence of our enemies.

STUDY QUESTIONS

> Study to shew thyself approved unto God, a workman that needeth not to be ashamed, rightly dividing the word of truth.
> — 2 Timothy 2:15

1. Have you ever wondered why God brings correction to your life? It's certainly a valid question many of us have, and God actually answers

it in His Word. Take a look at His words to the children of Israel in Deuteronomy 8:1-5 just before they entered the Promised Land, along with Jesus' words in John 15:2 and Paul's words in First Corinthians 11:32. What stands out to you?

2. Although people in the world might tell you otherwise, being corrected by someone who loves you and has your best interest at heart is one of the greatest gifts you could ever receive. What does the Bible have to say about receiving correction from God? Take a few moments to read what He says in Hebrews 12:5-13:

- God's discipline is a clear sign of two things: What are they?

- What do you receive from God when you cooperate with His discipline?

- According to this passage, how should you respond to the correction God gives?

(Also consider Proverbs 3:11,12 and Revelation 3:19.)

PRACTICAL APPLICATION

> But be ye doers of the word, and not hearers only,
> deceiving your own selves.
> —James 1:22

1. Stop and think: What would your life be like if God never corrected you? Consider how your children and grandchildren would be if they were never corrected.

2. God's correction is what ultimately keeps us safe from spiritual "wolves" and pulls us away from dangerous situations. Can you remember a time when His correction stopped you from making a mistake you would have seriously regretted?

3. When David was disciplined by the Lord, David owned up to his dreadful actions and did not run from God's chastisement. Is God trying to bring correction to your life? If so, what is it about? Are you making excuses for your behavior and fighting against His correction? Or are you admitting your errors and receiving His discipline?

LESSON 8

TOPIC
God's Supernatural Prosperity

SCRIPTURES
1. **Psalm 23:1-6** — The Lord is my shepherd; I shall not want. He maketh me to lie down in green pastures: he leadeth me beside the still waters. He restoreth my soul: he leadeth me in the paths of righteousness for his name's sake. Yea, though I walk through the valley of the shadow of death, I will fear no evil: for thou art with me; thy rod and thy staff they comfort me. Thou preparest a table before me in the presence of mine enemies: thou anointest my head with oil; my cup runneth over. Surely goodness and mercy shall follow me all the days of my life: and I will dwell in the house of the Lord for ever.
2. **Psalm 23:5** (*NLT*) — You prepare a feast for me in the presence of my enemies....
3. **Psalm 5:8** — Lead me, O Lord, in thy righteousness because of mine enemies; make thy way straight before my face.
4. **Psalm 6:7,10** (*NKJV*) — My eye wastes away because of grief; it grows old because of all my enemies.... Let all my enemies be ashamed and greatly troubled; let them turn back and be ashamed suddenly.
5. **Psalm 7:6** (*NKJV*) — Arise, O Lord, in Your anger; Lift Yourself up because of the rage of my enemies; Rise up for me to the judgment You have commanded!
6. **Psalm 7:15** (*NKJV*) — He made a pit and dug it out, And has fallen into the ditch which he made.
7. **Psalm 18:3,17,48** — I will call upon the Lord, who is worthy to be praised: so shall I be saved from mine enemies.... He delivered me from my strong enemy, and from them which hated me: for they were too strong for me.... He delivereth me from mine enemies: yea, thou liftest me up above those that rise against me....
8. **Psalm 25:2** (*AMPC*) — O my God, I trust, lean on, rely on, and am confident in You. Let me not be put to shame or [my hope in You] be disappointed; let not my enemies triumph over me.

9. **Psalm 25:19** (*NKJV*) — Consider my enemies, for they are many; And they hate me with cruel hatred.
10. **Psalm 27:2,6** — When the wicked, even mine enemies and my foes, came upon me to eat up my flesh, they stumbled and fell.... And now shall mine head be lifted up above mine enemies round about me...
11. **Psalm 27:11-12** (*AMPC*) — Teach me Your way, O Lord, and lead me in a plain and even path because of my enemies [those who lie in wait for me]. Give me not up to the will of my adversaries, for false witnesses have risen up against me; they breathe out cruelty and violence.
12. **Psalm 31:8** — (*NKJV*) And [You] have not shut me up [given me] into the hand of the enemy....
13. **Psalm 40:2** (*NKJV*) — He also brought me up out of a horrible pit, Out of the miry clay, And set my feet upon a rock, And established my steps.
14. **Psalm 41:2,11** (*AMPC*) — The Lord will protect him and keep him alive; he shall be called blessed in the land; and You will not deliver him to the will of his enemies.... By this I know that You favor and delight in me, because my enemy does not triumph over me.
15. **Psalm 55:23** (*NKJV*) — But You, O God, shall bring them down to the pit of destruction; Bloodthirsty and deceitful men shall not live out half their days; But I will trust in You.
16. **Psalm 57:6** (*NKJV*) — They have prepared a net for my steps; My soul is bowed down; They have dug a pit before me; Into the midst of it they themselves have fallen. Selah.
17. **Psalm 56:9** (*AMPC*) — Then shall my enemies turn back in the day that I cry out; this I know, for God is for me.
18. **Psalm 59:1** (*AMPC*) — Deliver me from my enemies, O my God; defend and protect me from those who rise up against me.
19. **Psalm 60:11** — Give us help from trouble: for vain is the help of man.
20. **Psalm 61:3** (*AMPC*) — For You have been a shelter and a refuge for me, a strong tower against the adversary.
21. **Psalm 64:1** (*AMPC*) — Hear my voice, O God, in my complaint; guard and preserve my life from the terror of the enemy.
22. **Psalm 71:13** (*AMPC*) — Let them be put to shame and consumed who are adversaries to my life....

23. **Psalm 91:3** (*NKJV*) — Surely He shall deliver you from the snare of the fowler, And from the perilous pestilence.
24. **Psalm 107:2** — Let the redeemed of the Lord say so, whom he hath redeemed from the hand of the enemy.
25. **Psalm 108:12,13** (*AMPC*) — Give us help against the adversary, for vain is the help of man. Through and with God we shall do valiantly, for He it is Who shall tread down our adversaries.
26. **Psalm 109:29** (*AMPC*) — Let my adversaries be clothed with shame and dishonor, and let them cover themselves with their own disgrace and confusion as with a robe.
27. **Psalm 118:5,6** (*NKJV*) — I called on the Lord in distress; The Lord answered me and set me in a broad place. The Lord is on my side; I will not fear. What can man do to me?
28. **Psalm 118:13** (*AMPC*) — You [my adversary] thrust sorely at me that I might fall, but the Lord helped me.
29. **Psalm 124:7** (*NKJV*) — Our soul has escaped as a bird from the snare of the fowlers; The snare is broken, and we have escaped.
30. **Psalm 138:7** (*AMPC*) — Though I walk in the midst of trouble, You will revive me; You will stretch forth Your hand against the wrath of my enemies, and Your right hand will save me.
31. **Psalm 143:9,12** (*AMPC*) — Deliver me, O Lord, from my enemies; I flee to You to hide me.... And in your mercy and loving-kindness, cut off my enemies and destroy all those who afflict my inner self, for I am Your servant.
32. **Psalm 144:6** (*AMPC*) — Cast forth lightning and scatter [my enemies]; send out Your arrows and embarrass and frustrate them.
33. **Proverbs 16:7** (*NKJV*) — When a man's ways please the Lord, He makes even his enemies to be at peace with him.
34. **1 Samuel 21:10-15** — And David arose, and fled that day for fear of Saul, and went to Achish the king of Gath. And the servants of Achish said unto him, Is not this David the king of the land? did they not sing one to another of him in dances, saying, Saul hath slain his thousands, and David his ten thousands? And David laid up these words in his heart, and was sore afraid of Achish the king of Gath. And he changed his behaviour before them, and feigned himself mad in their hands, and scrabbled on the doors of the gate, and let his spittle fall down upon his beard. Then said Achish unto his servants, Lo, ye see the man is mad: wherefore then have ye brought him to me? Have I

need of mad men, that ye have brought this fellow to play the mad man in my presence? shall this fellow come into my house?

35. **1 Kings 19:4-8** — ...And he requested for himself that he might die; and said, It is enough; now, O Lord, take away my life; for I am not better than my fathers. And as he lay and slept under a juniper tree, behold, then an angel touched him, and said unto him, Arise and eat. And he looked, and, behold, there was a cake baken on the coals, and a cruse of water at his head. And he did eat and drink, and laid him down again. And the angel of the Lord came again the second time, and touched him, and said, Arise and eat; because the journey is too great for thee. And he arose, and did eat and drink, and went in the strength of that meat forty days and forty nights unto Horeb the mount of God.

GREEK WORDS
There are no Greek words in this lesson.

SYNOPSIS
When we study the Scriptures, it is vital to understand the context in which a passage is written. Thus, in order to better grasp David's words in Psalm 23:5, we need to back up and read verse 4, which says, "Yea, though I walk through the valley of the shadow of death, I will fear no evil: for thou art with me; thy rod and thy staff they comfort me."

Clearly, David was describing a very challenging season. Circumstances and situations had become so dark that he compared them to "the valley of the shadow of death." Yet, even in the midst of this dreadful time, David recognized and declared the Lord's faithful provision: "Thou preparest a table before me in the presence of mine enemies..." (Psalm 23:5). Although experiencing a trouble-free life is impossible, trusting God to be faithful at all times is foolproof.

The emphasis of this lesson:

Regardless of how distressed or desperate our situation may be, we have God's guarantee of supernatural prosperity. Somehow and someway, He will move Heaven and earth to make sure we have what we need when we need it.

A Review of Psalm 23 and the Ten Promises of the Great Shepherd

The Bible says, "So then faith cometh by hearing, and hearing by the word of God" (Romans 10:17). When you hear God's Word again and again and again, it gets down deep inside your soul and spirit and fuels the fire of the Holy Spirit to empower your life on all levels. With that in mind, let's review Psalm 23 once more:

> The Lord is my shepherd; I shall not want. He maketh me to lie down in green pastures: he leadeth me beside the still waters. He restoreth my soul: he leadeth me in the paths of righteousness for his name's sake. Yea, though I walk through the valley of the shadow of death, I will fear no evil: for thou art with me; thy rod and thy staff they comfort me. Thou preparest a table before me in the presence of mine enemies: thou anointest my head with oil; my cup runneth over. Surely goodness and mercy shall follow me all the days of my life: and I will dwell in the house of the Lord for ever.
> — Psalm 23:1-6

This psalm of David is packed with ten powerful promises from God, including His guarantee of...

- **Supernatural provision (Psalm 23:1)**
- **Supernatural protection (Psalm 23:2)**
- **Supernatural peace (Psalm 23:2)**
- **Supernatural restoration (Psalm 23:3)**
- **Supernatural guidance (Psalm 23:3)**
- **Supernatural confidence (Psalm 23:4)**
- **Supernatural correction (Psalm 23:4)**
- **Supernatural prosperity (Psalm 23:5)**
- **Supernatural anointing/blessing (Psalm 23:5)**
- **Supernatural promise (Psalm 23:6)**

David's Journal of God's Faithfulness

Looking once more at Psalm 23:5, our key verse for this lesson, the *New Living Translation* says, "You prepare a feast for me in the presence of my enemies...." Enemies represent a threat. An enemy could be a person with ulterior motives who is conspiring against you or an overwhelming situation that appears to be your demise in some area. David was well-acquainted with such enemies throughout his life, and when you read through the book of Psalms, this reality becomes clear.

Again and again, David prayed to God concerning the adversaries he encountered. Look at and listen to what David wrote in these passages:

> **Psalm 5:8** — "Lead me, O Lord, in thy righteousness because of mine enemies; make thy way straight before my face."
>
> **Psalm 6:7,10 (*NKJV*)** — "My eye wastes away because of grief; it grows old because of all my enemies. Let all my enemies be ashamed and greatly troubled; Let them turn back and be ashamed suddenly."
>
> **Psalm 7:6 (*NKJV*)** — "Arise, O Lord, in Your anger; Lift Yourself up because of the rage of my enemies; Rise up for me to the judgment You have commanded!"
>
> **Psalm 7:15,16 (*NKJV*)** — "He [my enemy] made a pit and dug it out, and has fallen into the ditch which he made. His trouble shall return upon his own head, and his violent dealing shall come down on his own crown."

Jesus said, "...Out of the abundance of the heart the mouth speaks" (Matthew 12:34 *NKJV*). The fact that David mentions the topic of enemies so frequently is a clear indicator of what was dominating his thoughts...and prayers. Accordingly, he cried out for God to intervene.

> **Psalm 18:3,17,48** — "I will call upon the Lord, who is worthy to be praised: so shall I be saved from mine enemies.... He delivered me from my strong enemy, and from them which hated me: for they were too strong for me.... He delivereth me from mine enemies: yea, thou liftest me up above those that rise against me...."

Psalm 25:2 (*AMPC*) — "O my God, I trust, lean on, rely on, and am confident in You. Let me not be put to shame or [my hope in You] be disappointed; let not my enemies triumph over me."

Psalm 25:19 (*NKJV*) — "Consider my enemies, for they are many; and they hate me with cruel hatred."

Psalm 27:2,6 — "When the wicked, even mine enemies and my foes, came upon me to eat up my flesh, they stumbled and fell.... And now shall mine head be lifted up above mine enemies round about me...."

Even though David was experiencing one attack after another, he trusted in the Lord to deliver him from the hand of his enemies. In humility, he asked God to teach him, and in faith he declared victory over his adversaries.

Psalm 27:11,12 (*AMPC*) — "Teach me Your way, O Lord, and lead me in a plain and even path because of my enemies [those who lie in wait for me]. Give me not up to the will of my adversaries, for false witnesses have risen up against me; they breathe out cruelty and violence."

Psalm 31:7,8 (*NKJV*) — "I will be glad and rejoice in Your mercy, For You have considered my trouble; You have known my soul in adversities, And have not shut me up [given me] into the hand of the enemy...."

Psalm 40:2 (*NKJV*) — "He also brought me up out of a horrible pit, Out of the miry clay, And set my feet upon a rock, And established my steps."

Psalm 41:2,11 (*AMPC*) — "The Lord will protect him and keep him alive; he shall be called blessed in the land; and You will not deliver him to the will of his enemies.... By this I know that You favor and delight in me, because my enemy does not triumph over me."

Many times, David declared that his enemies would be swallowed by the very trap they had set for him.

Psalm 55:23 (*NKJV*) — "But You, O God, shall bring them down to the pit of destruction; Bloodthirsty and deceitful men shall not live out half their days; But I will trust in You."

> Psalm 57:6 (*NKJV*) — "They have prepared a net for my steps; My soul is bowed down; They have dug a pit before me; Into the midst of it they themselves have fallen. Selah."
>
> Psalm 56:9 (*AMPC*) — "Then shall my enemies turn back in the day that I cry out; this I know, for God is for me."
>
> Psalm 59:1 (*AMPC*) — "Deliver me from my enemies, O my God; defend and protect me from those who rise up against me."

One thing David never seemed to be concerned with was the thought of praying too much. His psalms clearly demonstrate — centuries in advance — Jesus' instruction to us to keep *asking*, *seeking*, and *knocking* until one's request is fulfilled (*see* Matthew 7:7-11).

> Psalm 60:11 — "Give us help from trouble: for vain is the help of man."
>
> Psalm 61:3 (*AMPC*) — "For You have been a shelter and a refuge for me, a strong tower against the adversary."
>
> Psalm 64:1 (*AMPC*) — "Hear my voice, O God, in my complaint; guard and preserve my life from the terror of the enemy."
>
> Psalm 71:13 (*AMPC*) — "Let them be put to shame and consumed who are adversaries to my life; let them be covered with reproach, scorn, and dishonor who seek and require my hurt."

Confidence in God's faithfulness to rescue him and execute justice on the wicked continually flowed from David's lips.

> Psalm 91:3 (*NKJV*) — "Surely He shall deliver you from the snare of the fowler, And from the perilous pestilence."
>
> Psalm 107:2 — "Let the redeemed of the Lord say so, whom he hath redeemed from the hand of the enemy."
>
> Psalm 108:12,13 (*AMPC*) — "Give us help against the adversary, for vain is the help of man. Through and with God we shall do valiantly, for He it is Who shall tread down our adversaries."
>
> Psalm 118:5,6 (*NKJV*) — "I called on the Lord in distress. The Lord answered me and set me in a broad place. The Lord is on my side; I will not fear. What can man do to me?"

Psalm 118:13 (*AMPC*) — "You [my adversary] thrust sorely at me that I might fall, but the Lord helped me."

Throughout his writings, David recognized God as the one who *revives*, the one who *makes a way of escape*, and the one who *delivers*. He repeatedly and unashamedly appealed to God to bring retribution against his enemies.

Psalm 109:29 (*AMPC*) — "Let my adversaries be clothed with shame and dishonor, and let them cover themselves with their own disgrace and confusion as with a robe."

Psalm 124:7 (*NKJV*) — "Our soul has escaped as a bird from the snare of the fowlers; the snare is broken, and we have escaped."

Psalm 138:7 (*AMPC*) — "Though I walk in the midst of trouble, You will revive me; You will stretch forth Your hand against the wrath of my enemies, and Your right hand will save me."

Psalm 143:9,12 (*AMPC*) — "Deliver me, O Lord, from my enemies; I flee to You to hide me.... And in your mercy and loving-kindness, cut off my enemies and destroy all those who afflict my inner self, for I am Your servant."

Psalm 144:6 (*AMPC*) — "Cast forth lightning and scatter [my enemies]; send out Your arrows and embarrass and frustrate them."

These verses from the book of Psalms are a mere sampling of all the passages that deal with adversaries, deliverance, and vengeance on the wicked. Without a doubt, David was thoroughly familiar with the subject. He also came to realize what his son Solomon would later write in the book of Proverbs: "When a man's ways please the Lord, He makes even his enemies to be at peace with him" (Proverbs 16:7 *NKJV*). It is the same principle of Psalm 23:5, "Thou preparest a table before me in the presence of mine enemies...."

God Met David's Needs in the Enemy Territory of Gath

There is a story from David's life recorded in First Samuel that places him right in the presence of one of his archenemies. As he was running from

King Saul who was trying to find David and kill him, he found himself in the very heartland of the Philistines. The Bible tells us:

> **And David arose, and fled that day for fear of Saul, and went to Achish the king of Gath. And the servants of Achish said unto him, Is not this David the king of the land? did they not sing one to another of him in dances, saying, Saul hath slain his thousands, and David his ten thousands? And David laid up these words in his heart, and was sore afraid of Achish the king of Gath.**
>
> **— 1 Samuel 21:10-12**

Stop and seriously consider what was taking place. David had been hand-picked by God and anointed as king of Israel. He was being hunted down by the man God had rejected — King Saul. Suddenly, he is standing before King Achish, the king of the Philistine city of Gath, the city from which Goliath came. Fearing for his life, David had to think and act fast. What did he do? Scripture says:

> **And he changed his behaviour before them, and feigned himself mad in their hands, and scrabbled on the doors of the gate, and let his spittle fall down upon his beard. Then said Achish unto his servants, Lo, ye see the man is mad: wherefore then have ye brought him to me? Have I need of mad men, that ye have brought this fellow to play the mad man in my presence? shall this fellow come into my house?**
>
> **— 1 Samuel 21:13-15**

The entire time David was in the territory of his enemies, God took care of him. Not only did He protect David, but He also fed him literally in the presence of his enemies. This is the same thing God did for David when he had first entered the service of King Saul who burned with jealousy against David.

God Supplied Supernatural Sustenance for Elijah When He Was Hunted by Jezebel

Another example of being cared for by the Lord in the presence of one's enemies is seen in the life of the prophet Elijah. After being the leader of an unprecedented move of God and witnessing the extermination of 450 wicked prophets of Baal, Elijah received a death threat from Queen

Jezebel and ran for his life into the wilderness. There he sat under a lone juniper tree, hopeless, exhausted, and totally depleted. The Bible says:

> …And he requested for himself that he might die; and said, It is enough; now, O Lord, take away my life; for I am not better than my fathers.
>
> And as he lay and slept under a juniper tree, behold, then an angel touched him, and said unto him, Arise and eat. And he looked, and, behold, there was a cake baken on the coals, and a cruse of water at his head. And he did eat and drink, and laid him down again.
>
> — 1 Kings 19:4-6

The depth of Elijah's depression was so severe that he fell right back to sleep. He was so depleted that a single serving of this supernatural food wasn't sufficient to replenish him. Consequently, the Bible says:

> And the angel of the Lord came again the second time, and touched him, and said, Arise and eat; because the journey is too great for thee. And he arose, and did eat and drink, and went in the strength of that meat forty days and forty nights unto Horeb the mount of God.
>
> — 1 Kings 19:7,8

Just as God did for David when he was surrounded by enemies, He also did for Elijah. The Lord literally set a table of food and drink in front of him when he was being hunted down by Jezebel. Not just once, but twice, God prepared a supernatural meal so that Elijah would have the energy and strength he would need to make the estimated 150-mile journey from Beersheba to Mount Horeb. It was a divine replenishing that invigorated his body, mind, and spirit.

Friend, Elijah and David are not the only people God promised to provide for. You, too, are guaranteed supernatural sustenance even in the midst of your adversaries. Realize that when you encounter enemies during your journey, you must learn to look for the table that your Shepherd has prepared for you. You don't have to wait for them to leave — God will give you a feast even in the presence of your enemies!

In our next lesson, we will examine the meaning of David's statement, "…Thou anointest my head with oil; my cup runneth over" (Psalm 23:5).

STUDY QUESTIONS

> Study to shew thyself approved unto God, a workman that needeth
> not to be ashamed, rightly dividing the word of truth.
> — 2 Timothy 2:15

1. Remember how David went to Gath — the very city Goliath was from — and received help when he was running from Saul. Isn't it amazing how God protected and provided for him and his men in the most unlikely place? What does this say to you about God's divine favor and protection for you? (Consider Acts 10:34; Romans 2:11 and 8:31,32.)
2. When Elijah was afraid and became depressed because of Jezebel's threat on his life, how did God respond to His prophet's pain, confusion, and exhaustion? How does seeing God's patient, caring response encourage you in your hard times? (Consider Matthew 12:20; Isaiah 40:11 and 42:3; Psalm 18:35,36.)
3. Many people in Scripture faced difficult times, including the prophet Habakkuk. Yet like David, he learned to encourage himself in the Lord's faithfulness and continue to put his trust in Him. Take time to reflect on the goodness of God in your own life (*see* Psalm 77:11-13), then read and reread this powerful declaration in Habakkuk 3:19 *AMPC*.

"The Lord God is my Strength, my personal bravery, and my invincible army; He makes my feet like hinds' feet and will make me to walk [not stand still in terror, but to walk] and make [spiritual] progress upon my high places [of trouble, suffering, or responsibility]!"

PRACTICAL APPLICATION

> But be ye doers of the word, and not hearers only,
> deceiving your own selves.
> — James 1:22

1. Who/what are the "enemies" that you are dealing with in your life? What provision are you needing from God and trusting Him to provide — even in the midst of challenging circumstances?
2. Think of a time you were in a situation like David or Elijah. Did you let yourself rest and enjoy the table God had prepared for you? If not, why? What do you know now about God's faithfulness that will help you rest, even in the presence of your enemies?

LESSON 9

TOPIC
God's Supernatural Anointing

SCRIPTURES
1. **Psalm 23:1-6** — The Lord is my shepherd; I shall not want. He maketh me to lie down in green pastures: he leadeth me beside the still waters. He restoreth my soul: he leadeth me in the paths of righteousness for his name's sake. Yea, though I walk through the valley of the shadow of death, I will fear no evil: for thou art with me; thy rod and thy staff they comfort me. Thou preparest a table before me in the presence of mine enemies: thou anointest my head with oil; my cup runneth over. Surely goodness and mercy shall follow me all the days of my life: and I will dwell in the house of the Lord for ever.
2. **1 Samuel 16:13** — Then Samuel took the horn of oil, and anointed him in the midst of his brethren: and the Spirit of the Lord came upon David from that day forward....
3. **2 Samuel 2:4** — And the men of Judah came, and there they anointed David king over the house of Judah....
4. **2 Samuel 5:3** — So all the elders of Israel came to the king to Hebron; and king David made a league with them in Hebron before the Lord: and they anointed David king over Israel.
5. **2 Corinthians 1:21** — Now he which [established] us with you in Christ, and hath anointed us, is God.

GREEK WORDS
1. "established" — βεβαιόω (*bebaioo*): firm, durable, dependable, or reliable; a legal term used to depict the lengthy and intensive investigative process involved to validate if a document was trustworthy
2. "anointed" — χρίω (*chrio*): to rub, to bathe, to massage; in most cases, it is used to depict the anointing of oil; in the Old and New Testament, it is primarily used to depict a person who is anointed with the Holy Spirit

SYNOPSIS

Have you ever heard someone say, "That man is an anointed preacher," or "That woman is an anointed singer"? It is a statement frequently made in many Christian circles. But what does it mean? Is the anointing something for every believer to experience or only a select few?

The good news is the anointing of God is available to everyone — including *you*! It is one of His supernatural promises to you as your Good Shepherd. In Psalm 23:5, David said of the Lord, "…Thou anointest my head with oil; my cup runneth over." When you are anointed by God, He personally places His hands on your life, and it becomes evident to all.

The emphasis of this lesson:

As God's child, He promises to anoint you with the "oil" of His Spirit until your cup runs over. This anointing is His promise to personally lay hands on your life and empower you to do extraordinary things. The imagery of your cup running over demonstrates God's extravagant love, welcoming you into His family.

The Old Testament speaks of a number of individuals who served as shepherds, including Moses and King Cyrus of Persia. Moses was a shepherd to the nation of Israel as they transitioned out of Egyptian bondage and made their way toward the Promise Land. And King Cyrus acted as a shepherd to Israel as they departed from Babylonian exile to rebuild the temple in Jerusalem (*see* Isaiah 44:28). Then there was David — the shepherd-boy anointed to be king — who wrote more than 70 psalms, including Psalm 23, which says:

> The Lord is my shepherd; I shall not want. He maketh me to lie down in green pastures: he leadeth me beside the still waters. He restoreth my soul: he leadeth me in the paths of righteousness for his name's sake. Yea, though I walk through the valley of the shadow of death, I will fear no evil: for thou art with me; thy rod and thy staff they comfort me. Thou preparest a table before me in the presence of mine enemies: thou anointest my head with oil; my cup runneth over. Surely goodness and mercy shall follow me all the days of my life: and I will dwell in the house of the Lord for ever.
>
> — Psalm 23:1-6

In this celebrated and cherished chapter of Psalms, God makes ten amazing promises. These include:

- **Supernatural provision (Psalm 23:1)**
- **Supernatural protection (Psalm 23:2)**
- **Supernatural peace (Psalm 23:2)**
- **Supernatural restoration (Psalm 23:3)**
- **Supernatural guidance (Psalm 23:3)**
- **Supernatural confidence (Psalm 23:4)**
- **Supernatural correction (Psalm 23:4)**
- **Supernatural prosperity (Psalm 23:5)**
- **Supernatural anointing/blessing (Psalm 23:5)**
- **Supernatural promise (Psalm 23:6)**

David Experienced Three Anointings

Immediately after David said, "Thou preparest a table before me in the presence of mine enemies," he added, "Thou anointest my head with oil; my cup runneth over" (Psalm 23:5). If anyone was familiar with the process of being anointed, it was David. The Bible actually records that he was anointed on three separate occasions.

The first time David was anointed was in the company of his brothers. First Samuel 16:13 states, "Then Samuel took the horn of oil, and anointed him in the midst of his brethren: and the Spirit of the Lord came upon David from that day forward...." This first anointing was done in a small environment with only a few of David's closest family members present. Nevertheless, from that day forward, something changed in David. The Spirit of the Lord came upon him, and those closest to him recognized it.

About 10 to 15 years later, David was anointed a second time while living in the city of Hebron. We find this recorded in Second Samuel 2:4, which states, "And the men of Judah came, and there they anointed David king over the house of Judah...." Here we see that the nation of Judah recognized the hand of God on David's life, so they anointed him as the king over all of Judah.

Shortly thereafter, David was anointed again — this time in the presence of all the tribes of Israel. Second Samuel 5:3 says, "So all the elders of Israel came to the king to Hebron; and king David made a league with them in Hebron before the Lord: and they anointed David king over Israel." With each anointing David experienced, there came a greater level of God's authority, and his sphere of influence was expanded.

We Must Be 'Established' Before We Are Anointed

David's life reveals that God gives His anointing to us in stages — one level of intensity at a time. This is confirmed by the apostle Paul in Second Corinthians 1:21 where he said, "Now he which [established] us with you in Christ, and hath anointed us, is God." Notice that being *established* comes *before* being anointed. That is what we see in the life of David.

You may be eager to get started with the vision or dream God has placed in your heart and wish things would begin moving faster. But you need to know that God is not focused on the clock like we usually are. Instead, He's more concerned about cultivating qualities such as character, integrity, faithfulness, and purity of heart. He must first establish a rock-solid foundation in you that will enable you to sustain the full work He wants to do in and through your life.

Perhaps you've heard the phrase, "Don't put the cart before the horse." Although many people struggle to keep these things in the right order, God doesn't. He isn't going to get the cart before the horse. Again, this is the principle articulated in Second Corinthians 1:21: "Now he which [established] us with you in Christ, and hath anointed us, is God."

The word "established" here is the Greek word *bebaioo*, which describes *something firm, durable, dependable, or reliable*. Thus, Paul is telling us that God must "establish" us first — He must make us *firm* in faith, *durable* to withstand any spiritual condition, and *steadfast, trustworthy, dependable*, and *reliable*. If you want God to anoint you and use you in a mighty way, you must possess these traits.

It takes firmness to stand for God. Anyone who is a leader must have durability to resist difficult, painful, awkward, or uncomfortable times. God must be assured that you are the kind of person on whom He can rely before He takes you to the next level of anointing.

Interestingly, the word *bebaioo* — translated here as "established" — is a legal term that was used to depict the lengthy and intensive investigative process involved to validate if a document was trustworthy and could be relied upon. In the ancient world, documents were written by hand. If those writing or copying the documents were not careful, mistakes could be made with serious legal consequences. For this reason, it was not wise to give one's final approval to a document until it was tested and proven trustworthy. Therefore, before a deal was finalized, the document was scrutinized to validate its reliability. If the document had errors in it, the errors had to be corrected before the papers were signed and the seal of approval was given to proceed. Once the document was "established" as valid, it could then be accepted and authorized.

This is what God does to us before He gives us greater anointings. Paul said, "Now he which [established] us with you in Christ, and hath anointed us, is God" (2 Corinthians 1:21). God does His due diligence to check us out and find out if we are durable, dependable, reliable, and trustworthy. If we are, He gives us a new, greater level of His anointing. This brings us to a very important question…

What Does It Mean To Be 'Anointed'?

The word "anointed" is a translation of the Greek word *chrio*, which means *to rub*, *to bathe*, or *to massage*. It is the root of the word *Christ*, which means *the Anointed One*. In most cases, the word *chrio* was used to depict the anointing of *oil*. Specifically, oil was used for anointing kings or those ordained into powerful positions. In the Old and New Testament, it's primarily used to depict a person who is anointed with the Holy Spirit. This was an act used for setting someone apart for a special, divine, or important purpose.

When a person was anointed with oil in ancient times, a prophet, a priest, a doctor, or a therapist would pour oil into his own hands. Once his hands were doused with oil, he would then place his hands on the person to be anointed and begin to massage or press the oil into the person's head, hair, or flesh. Oil was expensive and not to be wasted, so the idea of turning a bottle upside down and pouring its contents onto a person was non-existent. Oil was far too precious to be applied in such a manner.

Please realize that for a person to be anointed with oil, it required the anointer to put his hands on the one being anointed. It was impossible to be anointed without someone putting his hands on the recipient in order to apply the oil. Hence, in the truest sense, the word "anoint" describes a "hands-on" experience, and the moment hands were publicly laid on someone, it was seen as *endorsement* or *approval*.

For example, when elected officials were installed into office, the senior body of politicians publicly laid hands on each of them as a way of declaring that they were *officially endorsed* and therefore *empowered* to do their job. When hands were laid on a person, it was also *a public pronouncement of approval*. Similarly, in both Old and New Testament writings, the laying on of hands was used to declare *support* and *endorsement* of an individual.

Now let's take this truth and apply it to the principle we're studying in Second Corinthians 1:21. In this verse, we see God does *not* lay His hands on a person and thereby endorse him or her until He has first validated that the person is *trustworthy* of such an anointing. This act is so holy that God does not carry it out before doing "due diligence" to validate that a person is *trustworthy* of a greater anointing. To be clear, when a person is "anointed," it means God has laid His hands on him and the hand of God is on his life. This is what God did with David after He had tested him and found him to be durable, dependable, and trustworthy of greater anointing.

'My Cup Runneth Over'

After David tells us about the Lord anointing his head with oil, he adds, "…My cup runneth over" (Psalm 23:5). To grasp more fully what he is communicating here, we need to understand an important ancient-world custom. In biblical times when a person came into your home and you wanted to royally and lavishly welcome him, you would pour oil on his head until it was overflowing and running all over.

David's use of this ancient custom in connection with the anointing of the Lord tells us something extraordinary. He is saying our Shepherd receives us into His family lavishly and extravagantly! The Lord is so excited to welcome us into His flock that He pours out His oil in abundance all over us! Can you picture God having such a celebratory attitude toward you? Our cups overflow because of God's overflowing love for us.

Although the pessimist says, "My cup is half empty," and the optimist says, "My cup is half full," the true follower of Christ can proclaim, "My cup is running over!" Friend, God's love for you is overflowing! The Bible says,

"...The Holy One has anointed you and you all know the truth" (1 John 2:20 *TPT*). His desire is to progressively pour out greater levels of His anointing on your life to the point of overflow. If you want to experience these greater anointings, allow Him to prepare you and cooperate with what He is doing in your life.

In our final lesson, we will zero in on God's supernatural promise found in Psalm 23:6: "Surely goodness and mercy shall follow me all the days of my life: and I will dwell in the house of the Lord for ever."

STUDY QUESTIONS

> Study to shew thyself approved unto God, a workman that needeth not to be ashamed, rightly dividing the word of truth.
> — 2 Timothy 2:15

1. What new insights did you learn about the *anointing* of the Lord? How about the three anointings David experienced?
2. According to Mark 6:12 and 13, for what purpose did the twelve disciples use the anointing? What was the result? How does this relate to God's instructions to us in James 5:14 and 15?
3. As we learned, the word "anoint" describes a "hands-on" experience, and it has been connected with the act of publicly laying hands on individuals for thousands of years. Take a few moments to reflect on these examples in Scripture. What is the Holy Spirit showing you about the *laying on of hands* and the *anointing*?
   - Moses laying hands on Joshua (Numbers 27:18-20; Deuteronomy 34:9)
   - The Apostles laying hands on Stephen (Acts 6:1-8)
   - Paul laying hands on Timothy (1 Timothy 4:14; 2 Timothy 1:6,7)

PRACTICAL APPLICATION

> But be ye doers of the word, and not hearers only, deceiving your own selves.
> — James 1:22

1. David's life reveals that God gives His anointing to us *progressively* — one level of intensity at a time. Look back on your life. What unique

seasons can you identify that God brought you through? How was His anointing different in each season? What are some of the things you learned along your journey?

2. God wants to bring you into greater levels of His anointing, but first He has to establish His character in you. What Christ-like qualities can you see that God has already cultivated in you? What traits do you sense Him trying to develop in you right now? Pray and ask the Holy Spirit to show you anything you can do to better cooperate with His work in you.

3. Rather than just receiving a small sampling of God's anointing, the Bible says that your *cup runs over* (Psalm 23:5). This symbolizes His extravagant, overflowing love for you. How does picturing God's immense, celebratory love for you touch your heart?

LESSON 10

TOPIC
God's Supernatural Promise

SCRIPTURES
1. **Psalm 23:1-6** — The Lord is my shepherd; I shall not want. He maketh me to lie down in green pastures: he leadeth me beside the still waters. He restoreth my soul: he leadeth me in the paths of righteousness for his name's sake. Yea, though I walk through the valley of the shadow of death, I will fear no evil: for thou art with me; thy rod and thy staff they comfort me. Thou preparest a table before me in the presence of mine enemies: thou anointest my head with oil; my cup runneth over. Surely goodness and mercy shall follow me all the days of my life: and I will dwell in the house of the Lord for ever.

2. **Psalm 13:1-3** (*NKJV*) — How long, O Lord? Will You forget me forever? How long will You hide Your face from me? How long shall I take counsel in my soul, Having sorrow in my heart daily? How long will my enemy be exalted over me? Consider and hear me, O Lord my God; Enlighten my eyes, Lest I sleep the sleep of death.

3. **James 5:17** (*NLT*) — Elijah was as human as we are...

4. **Psalm 13:5,6** (*NKJV*) — But I have trusted in Your mercy; My heart shall rejoice in Your salvation. I will sing to the Lord, Because He has dealt bountifully with me.
5. **Psalm 103:1-6,8** — Bless the Lord, O my soul: and all that is within me, bless his holy name. Bless the Lord, O my soul, and forget not all his benefits: Who forgiveth all thine iniquities; who healeth all thy diseases; Who redeemeth thy life from destruction; who crowneth thee with lovingkindness and tender mercies; Who satisfieth thy mouth with good things; so that thy youth is renewed like the eagle's. The Lord executeth righteousness and judgment for all that are oppressed.... The Lord is merciful and gracious, slow to anger, and plenteous in mercy.
6. **Psalm 103:10-14** — He hath not dealt with us after our sins; nor rewarded us according to our iniquities. For as the heaven is high above the earth, so great is his mercy toward them that fear him. As far as the east is from the west, so far hath he removed our transgressions from us. Like as a father pitieth his children, so the Lord pitieth them that fear him. For he knoweth our frame; he remembereth that we are dust.
7. **Psalm 103:17,18** — But the mercy of the Lord is from everlasting to everlasting upon them that fear him, and his righteousness unto children's children; To such as keep his covenant, and to those that remember his commandments to do them.

GREEK WORDS
There are no Greek words in this lesson.

SYNOPSIS
Contrary to what you may have heard or what the enemy has tried to get you to believe, God only wants the very best for you at all times. He is not watching over you and waiting for you to mess up so He can bring correction. He is observing your life; looking and longing for opportunities to bless you! The Bible says, "And therefore the Lord [earnestly] waits [expecting, looking, and longing] to be gracious to you; and therefore He lifts Himself up, that He may have mercy on you and show loving-kindness to you..." (Isaiah 30:18 *AMPC*).

David understood this about the Lord, which is what prompted him to conclude Psalm 23 by saying, "Surely goodness and mercy shall follow me all the days of my life: and I will dwell in the house of the Lord for ever" (v. 6). Do you believe this? God wants you to. He has great things ahead for your life, and the more you believe it, the more you will receive the blessings He has prepared.

The emphasis of this lesson:

God's supernatural promise to you is that His goodness and mercy will follow you all the days of your life. Even when times of doubt arise and you're depleted of faith, God remains faithful to His promises.

A Review of What We've Learned

We have certainly covered a great deal of truth in the previous nine lessons regarding Psalm 23. One of the most important things you can receive from this study is to take this powerful passage — and the ten supernatural promises God declares — and make them your own. In other words, read each verse with personal emphasis. To help you, here is a personalized version of Psalm 23 in the *New King James Version*.

Read **Psalm 23:1** as, "The Lord is *MY* shepherd; *I* shall not want."

This is God's promise to you of **supernatural provision**.

Read **Psalm 23:2** as, "He makes *ME* to lie down in green pastures; He leads *ME* beside the still waters."

This is God's promise to you of **supernatural protection** and **supernatural peace**. With the Lord by your side, you can lie down and rest without fear because He is watching over you. He has given you His peace to permanently abide in your soul.

Read **Psalm 23:3** as, "He restores *MY* soul; He leads *ME* in the paths of righteousness for His name's sake."

This is God's promise to you of **supernatural restoration** and **supernatural guidance**. Through the power and Person of the Holy Spirit living inside of you, the Lord is always at work remaking the very core of your life. He is your personal tour guide who knows all the right roads you need to take and the ones to avoid.

Read **Psalm 23:4** as, "Yea, though *I* walk through the valley of the shadow of death, *I* will fear no evil; for You are with *ME*; Your rod and Your staff, they comfort *ME*."

This is God's promise to you of **supernatural confidence** and **supernatural correction**. Even in the darkest hours of your life, you can be confident you're going to make it through because the Lord is with you. He'll use His rod to protect you from predators and His staff to make sure you stay in line with His purpose for your life.

Read **Psalm 23:5** as, "You prepare a table before *ME* in the presence of *MY* enemies: You anoint *MY* head with oil; *MY* cup runs over."

This is God's promise to you of **supernatural prosperity** and **supernatural anointing**. It doesn't matter what threatening situations or evil people you face, God has got your back, and He will continue to provide the sustenance you need, right in the midst of your enemies. His anointing on your life increases progressively and affirms His hands-on involvement.

Read **Psalm 23:6** as, "Surely goodness and mercy shall follow *ME* all the days of *MY* life; and *I* will dwell in the house of the Lord forever."

This is God's **supernatural promise** to you, which is what we're going to cover in this lesson.

Like David, All of Us Have Moments of Doubt

Looking at Psalm 23:6, notice how David begins the verse with the word "surely." There is just something powerful about this word. There is no hesitation or uncertainty in David's voice. He is fully persuaded of God's promise to him — that God's goodness and mercy would follow him all the days of his life. David did not say *maybe*, *perhaps*, or "*I hope so.*" He declared — definitely, certainly, absolutely, indisputably, undoubtedly, unquestionably — that the blessings of God would always be his! This is the same promise that is available to you.

Now, you might think, *I wish I had the kind of confidence that David had. Sometimes I struggle with doubt.* It's tempting to think someone like David — especially after he penned such a powerful psalm — was always on the mountaintop or that he always had a perfect faith. But that was not the case. In fact, if we back up ten psalms, we see David in a much less confident frame of mind. Listen to what he says in Psalm 13:1-3 (*NKJV*):

> How long, O Lord? Will You forget me forever? How long will You hide Your face from me? How long shall I take counsel in my soul, Having sorrow in my heart daily? How long will my enemy be exalted over me? Consider and hear me, O Lord my God; Enlighten my eyes, Lest I sleep the sleep of death.

David doesn't sound very confident here, does he? It's wonderful when our faith is soaring and we feel energized and confident in God's Word, but we all have times of doubt and uncertainty. Thankfully, God is faithful to His promises even when we're depleted of faith and struggling to trust Him. Although we have a tendency to glorify biblical characters, the truth is, they all were real human beings just like us. At times they were frail, and they had flaws that were quite evident.

James confirms this. When he wrote about Elijah's powerful prayers, he prefaced it by saying, "Elijah was as human as we are…" (James 5:17 *NLT*). If you read the story of Elijah, you will see he was a powerful prophet, but he was also very moved by his emotions — even struggling at times with bouts of depression.

This same humanness is seen in David's life in the first few verses of Psalm 13. Yet, he didn't stay in doubt and discouragement. After his agonizing opening comments, he began to transition back into faith or what we might call the "victory side" of the equation. He said, "But I have trusted in Your mercy; My heart shall rejoice in Your salvation. I will sing to the Lord, Because He has dealt bountifully with me" (Psalm 13:5,6 *NKJV*).

Friend, don't let your flesh *or* the enemy condemn you when you experience times of frustration or questioning. It's normal. When your feelings begin to sink, just turn your eyes back on Jesus, and do your best to keep them there and continue to feed on His Word. He is your Great Shepherd. As you look to Him and remember His goodness and faithfulness, your faith will grow and your trust will soar.

David Gave Himself a Talking-To

As we've seen and noted throughout this study, David was no stranger to trials and life-threatening situations. Although he had many spiritual highs, he also experienced a number of lows. One of those moments of desperation took place about the time he wrote Psalm 103. God only knows what he was walking through at that moment. In any case, in the midst of his hopeless circumstances, he began to speak to his soul and say,

"Bless the Lord, O my soul: and all that is within me, bless his holy name" (Psalm 103:1).

Now, you may be familiar with this portion of Scripture, but don't hurry through it or you'll miss something extremely valuable. In this verse and the ones that follow, David is giving himself a major pep talk. He was speaking to his *soul* — his *mind*, *will*, and *emotions* — and telling himself to snap out of the doubt-filled, depressed spiral he was in and focus again on the goodness of God. He went on to say:

> **Bless the Lord, O my soul, and forget not all his benefits: Who forgiveth all thine iniquities; who healeth all thy diseases; Who redeemeth thy life from destruction; who crowneth thee with lovingkindness and tender mercies.**
> **— Psalm 103:2-4**

Apparently, David was being tempted to forget the benefits of serving the Lord, so he made himself remember things like God's power to heal and His amazing forgiveness. The word "forgive" here carries the idea of *permanently dismissing* or *sending something away without ever exercising the right to retrieve it again*. That is what God does with your sins when you ask Him to forgive you. David then said:

> **Who satisfieth thy mouth with good things; so that thy youth is renewed like the eagle's. The Lord executeth righteousness and judgment for all that are oppressed.... The Lord is merciful and gracious, slow to anger, and plenteous in mercy.**
> **— Psalm 103:5,6,8**

Aren't you grateful that God desires to satisfy you with good things, like healthy food to eat, clothes to wear, and a roof over your head? Aren't you glad that He is merciful and gracious and slow to anger? Where would we be without the mercy of God? Even when He is upset with us, David said:

> **He will not always chide: neither will he keep his anger for ever. He hath not dealt with us after our sins; nor rewarded us according to our iniquities. For as the heaven is high above the earth, so great is his mercy toward them that fear him. As far as the east is from the west, so far hath he removed our transgressions from us.**
> **— Psalm 103:9-12**

When God corrects us, He deals with us like a good father disciplines his children that He loves. Psalm 103:13 and 14 says, "Like as a father pitieth his children, so the Lord pitieth them that fear him. For he knoweth our frame; he remembereth that we are dust." This indicates that many of us are sometimes harder on ourselves and expect more of ourselves than even God does. Indeed, David declared:

> …The mercy of the Lord is from everlasting to everlasting upon them that fear him, and his righteousness unto children's children; To such as keep his covenant, and to those that remember his commandments to do them.
> — Psalm 103:17,18

Who are the blessings of God for? They are for everyone who obeys His commandments and keeps His covenant — including their children and grandchildren. Just think of all the benefits the Lord gives to you as you obey Him and live in relationship with Him. He provides:

- **Forgiveness of all your sins (Psalm 103:3)**
- **Healing from all your diseases (Psalm 103:3)**
- **Redemption from destruction (Psalm 103:4)**
- **Lovingkindness and tender mercies (Psalm 103:4)**
- **A life satisfied with good things (Psalm 103:5)**
- **Your youth renewed like the eagle's (Psalm 103:5)**
- **Righteousness and justice (Psalm 103:6)**
- **Mercy and grace (Psalm 103:8)**
- **Patience (Psalm 103:10)**
- **Forbearance (longsuffering) and forgiveness (Psalm 103:11)**
- **Forgetting and removing your sins (Psalm 103:12)**
- **Compassion (pity) for you (Psalm 103:13)**
- **Understanding of your human condition (Psalm 103:14)**
- **Faithfulness to His covenant with you (Psalm 103:18)**

When David was overwhelmed by the challenging circumstances he was facing, he forgot all these wonderful blessings from the Lord. To lift his spirit, he began to remind himself of all these things and then rehearse them aloud for his soul to hear and respond to God with praise.

God's Goodness and Mercy Are Chasing You Forever

This brings us back to Psalm 23:6 and David's confident declaration: "Surely goodness and mercy shall follow me all the days of my life: and I will dwell in the house of the Lord for ever." David emphatically and without question envisioned and believed two things would follow him all the days of his life: *God's goodness* and *God's mercy*. What's interesting is that the original Hebrew meaning of the word "follow" in this verse literally means to hunt down just like a hunter tracks down an animal.

David knew his connection with the Lord was a forever relationship! He knew he would spend eternity with His Shepherd. God was in it for the long-haul with David, and the same is true for us. We are in a forever relationship with the Creator of Heaven and Earth and will spend eternity with the Lord, our Good Shepherd!

STUDY QUESTIONS

Study to shew thyself approved unto God, a workman that needeth not to be ashamed, rightly dividing the word of truth.
— 2 Timothy 2:15

1. David was convinced and sure that God's goodness and mercy would follow him all the days of his life — right into eternity. What does that speak to you about God's love for us? Carefully read Romans 8:35-39 for some natural — and supernatural — examples of what can never stop God's love and goodness from finding you.

2. What happens if we are unfaithful? Does our unfaithfulness negate God's Word and prevent Him from being faithful to us? Consider Romans 3:3 and 4; Second Timothy 2:13; Psalm 146:6; and Deuteronomy 7:9 as you answer.

3. Each time David was faced with the temptation to quit, he remembered God's faithfulness to him. When Jesus faced the temptation to quit and abandon God's plan (as we all do), how did He respond? Read Matthew 4:1-11 (and Luke 4:1-13) for the answer. What can you learn from Jesus' example and apply in your own life?

PRACTICAL APPLICATION

> But be ye doers of the word, and not hearers only,
> deceiving your own selves.
> —James 1:22

1. Think about your own life and all the ways God has redeemed you from destruction. What would your life be like had He never saved you? Where might you be today? Of all the blessings you have received, for which ones are you most grateful?

2. Now imagine what your life would be like with God's goodness and mercy chasing you down. What specific things can you see yourself being able to do, knowing that God and all of Heaven are backing you?

3. Take some time to share with God what you're thinking about and how you're feeling — the good, the bad, and the ugly. If He can handle David's honesty, He can handle yours. Journal what you want to tell God — or even what you wish He and others really understood about you — in the space below. How does knowing you can be gut-level honest with God change your view of your relationship with Him?

4. Have you ever given yourself a pep talk to encourage your soul? If so, what was going on in your life at that time? How did God prove Himself faithful and deliver you or bring you through that situation? How does the memory of God's lovingkindness in your life give you hope that He will bring you out of the struggle you're currently facing?

Notes

Notes

Printed in the USA
CPSIA information can be obtained
at www.ICGtesting.com
LVHW011327111124
796290LV00006B/318